THE
OPEN LEARNING
HANDBOOK

THE OPEN LEARNING HANDBOOK

Selecting, Designing and
Supporting Open Learning Materials

Phil Race

Kogan Page, London/Nichols Publishing, New York

First published in 1989 by Kogan Page Ltd
120 Pentonville Road, London N1 9JN

Typeset by DP Photosetting, Aylesbury, Bucks
Printed and bound in Great Britain by
Biddles Ltd, Guildford

British Library Cataloguing in Publication Data

Race, Phil
    The open learning handbook
    1. Distance study
    I. Title
    371.3

ISBN 1-85091-833-3

First published in the United States of America
in 1989 by Nichols Publishing, an imprint of
GP Publishing Inc., PO Box 96, New York, NY 10024

Library of Congress Cataloguing in Publication Data

Race, Philip.
    The open learning handbook: selecting, designing, and supporting
open learning materials/Philip Race.
        p.   cm.
    ISBN 0-89397-341-6: $32.50
    1. Distance education.   2. Correspondence schools and courses.
I. Title.
LC5800.R3   1989
371.3--dc19

Contents

Acknowledgements   9
Foreword   11

1 WHAT IS OPEN LEARNING?   13
   I   *Open Learning: Practices and Principles*   14
      Section objectives   14
      Open learning or distance learning?   14
      How does open learning work?   14
      Conclusions   20

   II *Open Learning versus Traditional Textbooks*   21
      Section objectives   21
      Features and comparisons   21
      Conclusions   25

   III *Using Open Learning in Face-to-Face Courses*   26
      Section objectives   26
      Mix and match   26
      Which learners are particularly helped?   29
      Conclusions   30

2 MAKING OBJECTIVES USEFUL TO OPEN LEARNERS   32
      Aim   32
      Objectives   32
      What is an 'aim'?   32
      What is an 'objective'?   33
      Whose objectives should they be?   36
      Why design objectives for open learners?   36
      How can objectives help writers?   38
      Mapping out objectives   38
      Making objectives useful to open learners   38
      Checklist   40
      Conclusions   41

3 COMPOSING SELF-ASSESSMENT QUESTIONS AND
  RESPONSES   42
    Objectives   42
    What is a self-assessment question?   42
    What is the role of the SAQ response?   43
    What purposes should SAQs and responses serve?   45
    How best can SAQs and responses serve their purposes?   46
    Types of SAQ   46
    SAQ quality control   57
    Conclusions   59

4 STRATEGIES FOR WRITING   60
    Objectives   60
    Why do we need to think about strategies?   60
    What comes first?   61
    When can I design assignment material?   63
    When can I write some text?   64
    The introduction   65
    Reviews, summaries, checklists   65
    Visual material   66
    Choosing and using non-print media   67
    Checklist for medium 'X'   68
    Signposting   69
    Conclusions   73

5 USER-FRIENDLY TONE AND STYLE   75
    Objectives   75
    The arguments for and against   75
    How can you measure your tone and style?   77
    Conclusions   80

6 TUTOR-MARKED ASSIGNMENTS   81
    Objectives   81
    What purposes should assignments serve?   82
    What are the tools in an assignment toolkit?   82
    Feedback versus scores/grades   82
    What do learners look for first?   84
    What can we do about scores and feedback?   84
    Design of tutor-marked assignments   85
    TMAs are serious stuff   86
    Designing a marking scheme   87
    Improving assignments during piloting   89
    Conclusions   90

7 COMPUTER-MARKED ASSIGNMENTS   91
    Objectives   91

What is a computer-marked assignment? 91
What bits make up a CMA? 92
Scores 93
Other uses of CMAs 94
Conclusions 97

8 SELLING THE BENEFITS OF OPEN LEARNING 98
Objectives 98
What are the main features of open learning? 98
The market 99
Why all this emphasis on 'selling the benefits'? 102
Conclusions 104

9 HOW TO TUTOR OPEN LEARNERS 105
Objectives 105
What's involved in tutoring? 105
Do open learners need tutoring? 106
Who are open learners? 106
Making your own learner profiles 107
How does the open learner feel at the beginning? 107
Learners' needs in mid-course 108
Learners' needs towards the end of the course 109
Why concentrate on the negative feelings? 109
How can a good tutor help? 110
Conclusions 114

10 INTERACTIVE HANDOUTS – OPEN LEARNING
PROCESSES IN THE LECTURE ROOM 115
Objectives 115
The lecture situation 115
Lectures: content versus processes? 116
Some problems with lectures 117
Interactive materials and processes 118
Conclusions 123

11 ADULT ENTRY TO SCIENCE AND TECHNOLOGY 124
Objectives 124
Problems adults experience when beginning to learn science
and technology subjects 125
Some answers and remedies 126
Conclusions 128

12 EDITING OPEN LEARNING MATERIALS 129
Objectives 129
Educational editing 129
How *not* to do an educational edit 130

Checklist for educational editing   131
Conclusions   133

13 CHOOSING AND USING OPEN LEARNING   135
Checklist areas   135
Interaction   135
Objectives   136
Text: tone and style   136
Diagrams etc   137
Study skills help   137
Use of media   137
Assessment   138
Miscellaneous key issues   138
Conclusions   139

14 OPEN LEARNING: A CATALYST FOR STAFF
DEVELOPMENT   140
Objectives   140
Close encounters with open learning   140
Staff development implications   141
Conclusions   146

15 WORKSHOPS THAT WORK   147
A specimen workshop programme   147
A specimen discussion paper   148
So what actually happened at the workshop?   152
A specimen open learning workshop programme   152
Conclusions   154

Index   155

Acknowledgements

I'm pleased to share the blame for this book – and my thanks – with countless participants at my workshops during the last few years; I thank them for numerous ideas, suggestions, and arguments. My thanks are earned by John Simms for numerous wise suggestions (and whose influence pervades Chapter 15), John Coffey (Principal of Wolsey Hall, Oxford) for inspiration and encouragement, and by Dr John Cowan (Scottish Director, the Open University) for many very helpful (and sobering) perceptions (particularly in Chapter 14). I am also grateful to Dr John Davies (Director of the Polytechnic of Wales) and Clem Roberts (Deputy Director) for their encouragement and for enabling me to get on with writing this book.

Phil Race, September 1988

Foreword

I've written this book for people who are involved in open learning in various ways (such as authors, tutors, counsellors, editors and so on), and also for people who may be moving into the field of open learning for the first time.

I've tried to use the sort of informal, user-friendly language which is now being found desirable in many open learning materials. If you don't like plain-speaking, and prefer things written in sophisticated language, this book isn't meant for you.

Though my tone and style may be simple (I hope you'll agree) I've made no compromises regarding quality criteria. Most chapters contain lists of such criteria in one form or another, and only the best open learning materials (and tutors) presently live up to some of the criteria I've proposed. I hope that this book may help to rectify this situation.

This book isn't an open learning package. People are always saying to me 'Why not show us how to do it, by writing an open learning package about open learning?' Many authors (including myself) have tried to do this – but I don't think any of our attempts has been entirely successful. One reason is that this book would be three times thicker (and three times the price) if every issue was covered using self-assessment questions and responses. Another reason is that each reader needs to select and adapt ideas from a book such as this, and develop them for particular purposes, and particular learners. So this book is meant as a starting point, not a package for you to 'complete'.

Why call this a 'Handbook'? I've tried to cover the key things that people need to consider about the various aspects of open learning that I've addressed. I've also aimed to make this book self-contained and self-sufficient. There are no references to the literature! This is because the literature is now so big – and often disagrees with itself! Too much of it has been written by people whose feet are some way from the ground. Besides, if you spend all your time and energy reading the literature, you'll have none left to get moving with open learning.

1. What is Open Learning?

This chapter is in three main sections:

- An introduction to some of the practices and principles of open learning
- A comparison of good open learning materials with the more traditional textbook or instruction manual
- An exploration of some of the ways in which the advantages of open learning systems can be realized in traditional face-to-face courses.

I. Open Learning: Practices and Principles

Section objectives

When you've studied this section, you'll be able to:

1. Explain to other people how open learning works.
2. See how the skills of teachers and trainers can be directed towards helping open learners.
3. Put open learning into perspective – as 'nothing new'!

Open learning or distance learning?

In this book, we're looking at 'open' learning. However, there's another term that we'd better clarify first: 'distance learning'. What's the difference between distance learning and open learning?

Open learning can certainly be done at a distance. For example, thousands of Open University students work on their own for most of the time they study, rarely attending any sort of live session. Also, thousands of correspondence students work on their own, periodically sending assignments to distant tutors for assessment and comment.

However, open learning can also happen in a crowded lecture room. Suppose the lecturer asks the class to spend a few minutes digging in some handout materials for the answers to some questions posed to the class; the class members work on their own for a while – open learning. Similarly, open learning can occur in laboratories, training centres, workshops – just about anywhere. It doesn't matter whether the learner is part of a group or on his or her own, open learning can still be happening.

So, we don't need to worry too much about the term 'distance learning'. The important thing is that the environment and learning materials are causing *effective* learning to happen, whether or not the learner is at a distance from the provider.

How does open learning work?

First, let's clarify what people mean when talking about open learning. Below I've listed some of the questions I'm often asked about open learning, and I've given comments reflecting my personal answers to the questions.

What does 'open' mean in 'open learning'?
It means that the learner (or trainee, or student) has *choice*. He or she has freedom to manoeuvre. The learner has more control. There isn't as much control imposed by such people as lecturers, instructors, or teachers as in conventional training and education.

'Open' can also sometimes refer to entry criteria. Many open learning programmes attempt to dispense with strict prerequisite qualifications or experience (though of course it is very necessary for learners to be aware of what they should already be able to do before starting on such a programme).

What kinds of choice and control do open learners have?

They have more control over the pace they're going to work at. They can take as long as is needed to complete a chunk of studying. No more getting bored because the lecturer is going too slow. No more losing track because the lecturer is going too fast. When in open learning mode, learners have control of the rate of studying – but of course they also have the responsibility associated with making the choice a sensible one. There may still be deadlines to meet – target-dates for written assignments, and even exam dates. However, the slow learner can still enjoy freedom of pace simply by putting in more hours than the rapid learner, and meet the same deadlines.

Open learners may choose *where* to learn. Open learning can be done at home, or in a library, or at the workplace, or just about anywhere.

Open learners can choose *when* to do their learning. This can mean that they learn much more effectively than they might have done at 'imposed' time slots. In face-to-face courses, how many students look bleary-eyed in morning lectures? This may be because they come to life at night rather than in the morning! With open learning, night owls can choose to do their work at night.

Open learners can also choose *how* to learn. What I mean here is that they can choose – for example – to plan out a programme of 'targets' regarding the completion of the open learning programme. The learners can choose to revise systematically. They can deliberately go back over the harder bits – as many times as is needed to get them sorted out properly.

What's an open learning package?

There are all sorts of things that can be called open learning packages. Some are entirely made up of printed material. The best print-based packages are quite different from the average textbook, however; we'll explore the differences later in this chapter. Many open learning packages use audio tapes, video recordings, computer software and so on. So, basically, an open learning package can have many forms – the common factor is that learners can work through the package on their own.

Is open learning as good as conventional training?

This much-asked question implies that conventional training is always good. I'm sure you'd admit that much of the training you've had in the past was not perfect? When compared with 'average' training, open learning (at its best) is probably much better in fact! (I'd better emphasize that I'm talking about *good quality* open learning – good materials, effective learner support, and so on. Throughout this book you'll find criteria to help you sort out exactly which open learning materials may be ranked among the best.)

What's new about open learning?

Think back for a moment. Where did *you* do your learning? The real learning I mean. Was it done in classrooms, lecture rooms, and so on? Or was the real learning done *later* when you got down to it *on your own*, armed with the *notes* that you took from the classrooms?

In fact, can't you remember learning things as exams loomed up, months after the lectures concerned – when the lectures themselves were so far back that you couldn't remember anything about them – apart from your notes? Was there any lecturer or trainer standing over you when you did most of the *real* work? Or were you working in your own way, at your own pace, *on your own*?

Do you see what I'm getting at? I'm arguing that most of your real learning happened by what we're now calling *open learning* methods. I'd go as far as to say that open learning is the *natural* way that most learning has happened through the ages. Galileo is reported to have said: 'You can't teach a man anything, you can however help him to learn.' It's true than no one can do our learning for us. I think it's fair to say that learning is something we do by ourselves, even when learning from other people. A good open learning package is simply something that is designed to make best use of our natural way of learning things.

So why is open learning (at its best) so good?

Well, for a start, there may be far less time wasted. For example, time – and expense – travelling to and from classrooms (or training centres) may be eliminated or reduced.

But, more important, open learners don't have to sit there being trained in things they already know perfectly well. It's reckoned that, on average, for more than half of the time learners spend on conventional training courses, they're being taught stuff they already know! True, there are going to be some in a group who *don't* know it, but how sad for all the rest who already do. Now with an open learning package, learners can skim very quickly over stuff they already know adequately, and slow down to *concentrate* as soon as something new comes up.

In lectures, it's not very easy to control the pace at which each member of the group learns! In fact, it's possible for some of them to learn very little! If you're teaching a group of 30, for example, at any moment in time you may be lucky to have two or three of them 'with you', with others thinking ahead of you – and others not thinking much at all! With an open learning package, each learner is thinking at his or her own pace.

But what if parts of the learning package are irrelevant to learners' needs?

You may well decide to use an open learning package that isn't 'spot on' the subjects you want your students to learn. (This can well be preferable to taking the time to write something specially for them.) Ask yourself this, now: is each conventional lecture relevant to the needs of each individual learner? At best, a session may meet the needs of the complete group of learners present, but not *every* learner will need each element.

With an open learning package, each learner can home in on those parts directly relevant to his or her present needs. The package can be retained for things which may be needed later. And if anything is totally irrelevant, the open learner can skip it. (Much less embarrassing than going to sleep during an irrelevant bit of a live session!)

So the lecturer (or trainer) is now redundant?

Far from it. A human being can do all sorts of things vital to the success of any learner. Things such as dealing with each learner's individual problems (they all have different ones). Things that we often would like to do, but time doesn't allow. The human side of open learning needs people who:

- can be counsellors, fine-tuning the learning programme to the different needs and capabilities of learners
- can select the learning modules which will be most beneficial
- can assess learners' work on the modules
- can encourage and motivate learners
- can deal with individual problems on an individual basis.

Those supporting open learners can devote energy to all those things that need human skills and sensitivity. Teachers or trainers have time to do this when freed from much of the mere information-passing of conventional training. The open learning package itself does most of the routine information-giving.

People supporting open learners can be available at set times for individual students who need help with their open learning studies. If Fred comes along with a problem, Fred gets the help he needs. If Fred asked his question in a lecture, everyone else would have to wait as Fred's problem was dealt with.

In short, as supporters of open learners we can be *resources*, rather than 'transmitters' of information. We may in fact be very good at 'transmitting' – but in the lecture situation how switched on are our students as 'receivers'?

Most of the subsequent chapters in this book explore ways in which people can (1) infuse their skills into the design of open learning programmes, and (2) use their human qualities to enhance the learning experiences of open learners.

No more live sessions?

Live sessions are still very useful, but when incorporated as part of an open learning programme, they can be devoted to the things that are *best* done live. Things such as dealing with questions, developing practical skills, sharing ideas, discussing and debating, group analysis – all things where the learners *participate* rather than simply *receive*. Live sessions can be particularly useful *after* learners have done some open learning about background material; the sessions can then *build* on their learning. Live sessions may well be fewer, but their value to each learner will be greatly increased.

But surely there are things that can't be learned by learners on their own?

Of course there are. There are all sorts of things that are best learned through discussion and interaction. They can be dealt with in live sessions. However, in just about every subject, there are sections of theory, background material, practice exercises, and exploration that *can* be done by the learners under their own steam. So, the solution is quite simple: use open learning for the things it does best, and save human resources for the things that really need human skills.

Is open learning cost-effective?

Certainly there *are* costs. Materials may need to be purchased, or it may be necessary to produce brand new packages if existing materials don't measure up to the learners' needs. However, there are savings as well as costs.

Travelling to and from a college or training centre may be reduced, saving time as well as money. Accommodation costs may be substantially reduced; for example, when part of the study programme is done at home. For people in employment, 'time off the job' may be substantially reduced. Moreover, experience shows that most open learners tend to take their materials home with them, even if their firm allows company time for their studies. This means that studying is being done out of paid hours – an obvious bonus for employers!

Even in conventional college courses, using open learning as an integral component of courses can bring savings: less pressure on lecture room provision, and more availability to help people as individuals. However, 'cost effective' involves effectiveness as well as cost! If students learn something more effectively by open learning, surely that in itself helps to justify any extra costs involved.

How well does open learning 'stick'?

Do the benefits of having studied something as an open learner continue, long after the studies are completed? Indeed they do. For example, when learners are able to retain their learning materials, they have their 'trainer' right there anytime they need to brush-up or revise. The same can't be said of notes and materials acquired during conventional training – years later these may be quite insufficient to allow learners to recall the essence of the training sessions.

Also, any good open learning module will contain a lot more detail than a set of handwritten notes. In a live lecture, it's not usually possible to write more than a few pages of notes. In the same hour or so, an open learner may be able to work through quite a lot of pages of a module.

The fundamental difference is that a good open learning package *does* much of the training. Its owner therefore has the original 'trainer' on tap at any time when some revision is needed.

But what if learners can't retain the learning materials?

With computer-based systems, interactive video, and so on, learners won't normally be able to 'own' the learning resources. However, they will usually be able to return to the systems to brush up their knowledge. When they return, they have the advantage of revising from exactly the same resources that they used in their initial learning – and of course can re-learn very quickly.

What does it feel like being an open learner?
Firstly, back to another question: 'What does it feel like being trained in conventional training situations?' Be honest, how many of us actually enjoy being at the receiving end of teaching? How many of us often feel a bit patronized – or even 'put down'?

A good open learning programme gives the learner the feeling *'I'm getting there under my own steam'*. The open learner can enjoy much of the credit for each new skill developed. It hasn't been *given* by some other person. Things we learn under our own steam seem to stay with us for much longer than things we were taught by other people. We have a feeling of 'ownership' of things we learned under our own steam.

Having a good tutor can make a big difference to what it feels like being an open learner – we'll explore this in detail later in the book.

Has open learning no disadvantages?
Well, yes. For a start, learners studying entirely alone do miss out on the help they would have had from fellow learners in a group. For example, when Fred asks a question during a lecture, there may have been several of his colleagues who didn't know the answer to the question – or who didn't even realize that knowing the answer to that question was important. Also, learners in a group get useful information about how well (or otherwise) they are getting on, by comparing their performance with that of colleagues.

Furthermore, that spark of inspiration that is generated by the best lecturers, may be missed out on by the open learner. However, how many lecturers are as good as the best? Can *you* remember as many really inspiring teachers of lecturers as you can remember rather 'ordinary' (to be kind!) ones?

If open learning is combined with group sessions, of course, we can have the best of both worlds. In the final section of this chapter, we'll explore circumstances in 'conventional' courses where it may be desirable to have students learning in self study mode, rather than in lecture rooms. When using open learning it is indeed important to select the most appropriate topics for students to learn on their own. There will often be topics which really do need human teaching skills to be learned effectively.

How can I tell whether the open learning method is really working?
There's a lot of experience about now concerning how best to evaluate open learning programmes. You can get evidence of the learners' performance through tests and assessments – and monitor improvements. Even more important, however, you'll need the learners' side of things. Their views, impressions, feelings and reactions can be collected, through questionnaires, or interviews.

What sort of long-term future has open learning?

Though the term 'open learning' is relatively recent, I hope you're now convinced that open learning has been going on for a very long time! It's not a 'flash in the pan' or a 'flavour of the month'. There's a strong current in the direction of greater learner-centredness. I'd go as far as to predict that the trend towards open learning will continue until the majority of post-school education and training will be using open learning methods for some (sometimes all) of the programme content.

That doesn't mean the end of live training courses – but it does mean that live courses will be concentrating much more on those things where the physical presence of the trainer or lecturer is crucial. All sorts of areas not requiring such physical presence (background information, theory, practice, applications, and so on) will be studied in open learning mode, with learners enjoying the benefits of being able to work at their own pace, and at times and places which fit naturally into their daily routines (whether at home or at work).

Learners will also be enjoying the substantial benefits associated with being able to measure their own progress. A cynic said to me recently: 'The advantage of open learning is that it provides privacy within which to fail!' There is some truth in this; the open learner can get things wrong, then sort things out for himself using the feedback provided in the open learning materials. This can all happen without the humiliation of having been seen to make mistakes. And it provides a good way of finding out what the likely mistakes are, and how to avoid making them in future when it really matters – perhaps in exams.

Conclusions

Open learning can:

- open up various choices and degrees of control to learners
- use materials which are learner-centred
- allow learners to take credit for their learning
- help conserve human skills for things that really need human presence.

II. Open Learning versus Traditional Textbooks

Section objectives

By the end of this section, you'll be able to:

- list the main quality features of the best open learning materials
- discuss why learning from open learning materials can be much more productive than learning from textbooks.

The fact that you're reading this book probably means that you've had a lot of experience with textbooks in your life. In fact, you've probably become rather expert at working with textbooks. However, many people who need training aren't textbook experts. That's why most good open learning materials are considerably different from textbooks – even when open learning materials are entirely print-based.

The best of the modern generation of open learning materials are different in many ways from the 'bad, old, traditional textbook'. Below I present a comparison of the features of open learning materials and textbooks. This comparison is mainly based on the different degrees of learner-centredness of the two genres. I am of course aware that the features of open learning materials I list below are those of the *very best* of such materials. Also, many modern textbooks are not representative of the 'bad' features I mention for textbooks below!

However, even with these reservations, the worst thing that can be said about some open learning material is that it is 'textbookish'! Therefore, when selecting and evaluating open learning materials, criteria such as those mentioned below will be useful.

Features and comparisons

Content

Open learning materials are *interaction-centred*; it's what the learner *does* that really matters. Learning happens by 'having a go'.

Textbooks tend to be content-centred; the content is the be-all and end-all.

Motivation

Open learning materials are written so as to get the learner interested and involved. The learner may already be highly motivated, or alternatively may have been instructed to do the learning concerned by a superior at work.

Textbooks often assume (perhaps wrongly) that the reader is already interested. How many textbooks spend much of their lives unopened on shelves?

Self-esteem

Open learning materials (especially the best ones) cultivate and develop the self-esteem of learners. Learners are given the framework within which to think things out for themselves; they then have much more 'ownership' of the skills and knowledge they develop.

The average textbook merely presents its reader with information; readers don't benefit from a feeling of 'ownership' of their progress.

Relevance

Most open learning materials are purpose-built to be wholly relevant to the needs of a target group of learners.

Many textbooks tend to concentrate on the things the authors wished to present. Only certain sections of the average textbook are directly relevant to any individual learner. Students are often lacking in the essential skill of being able to track down the relevant parts of textbooks. Few realize how useful contents-pages and index sections can be for this purpose.

Ego trips

A good open learning module gives the successful learner a confidence boost. The learner feels he or she can take much of the credit for the newly acquired skills and knowledge. Much of the learning has occurred in an experiential way, through having a go at self-assessment questions or assignments, then benefiting from the feedback provided in the learning materials. When learners get things wrong, their mistakes are made in private – much less daunting than in public. Don't we all learn much from our mistakes?

It can often be said of textbooks that it is the author who has taken the ego trip.

Structure

Open learning materials are structured to meet the learners' needs. The author's original drafts may be changed quite drastically during editing and after piloting, so that learners are as well served as possible.

Most textbooks have structures which were largely provided by the authors. Few textbooks are piloted in the same way as good open learning modules are; nor are they adjusted radically to meet learners' needs.

Questions and answers

Open learning materials include many questions, particularly self-assessment questions. The best open learning materials don't just have answers to such questions; they have *responses*. A response is much better than a mere answer – a response may help the learner find out (in private) exactly *why* he or she made particular mistake, for example. We'll explore self-assessment in detail in Chapter 3.

Many textbooks have questions and answers, but relatively few readers actually attempt the questions. For those who do there may be little help if they don't manage to get the right answer first time.

Assumptions and errors
When an open learner makes a false assumption or error, the good open learning module will quickly show what this was, and why it happened. Self-assessment questions are designed to show learners whether they are making any such assumptions or errors.

With textbooks, it may be only too easy to press on carrying false assumptions, leading to erratic learning.

Objectives
Open learning materials use objectives to help learners see exactly what they're supposed to become able to do. The objectives also provide learners with the means to test how they're getting on. We'll explore some of the finer points regarding objectives in Chapter 2.

Textbooks sometimes give objectives, but they're rarely turned into an active and useful part of the way the reader is directed to handle the information presented.

Tone and Style
Most open learning materials use 'friendly' language. The learner becomes 'you'. The author is 'I'. The learner feels part of what is going on. We'll look at 'tone and style' aspects in detail in Chapter 5.

Textbooks are usually written in the third person passive style. The tone is objective, but remote – and often boring.

White space
Many print-based open learning modules leave white space for learners to write in. Learners may also be ticking boxes, adding to diagrams, filling in numbers in tables, and so on. Computer-based open learning materials often allow learners to enter things via the keyboard. All this adds to the involvement of the learners (even working on their own). The learning materials soon begin to 'belong' to the learners much more, due to all the things they write or draw into them.

Textbooks often cram every available space on each page with information – text, figures, tables and so on.

Active visuals
In open learning materials, when diagrams, graphs, tables, charts and so on are used, they are used *actively*. Learners are asked to do things with them. Learners use them, add to them, interpret them, pick out trends, and so on.

In textbooks, diagrams, graphs, tables, charts and so on are simply there. The reader may or may not take much notice of them.

Visuals: expectations?
In open learning materials, learners will usually be told exactly what the intention is regarding things like diagrams, graphs, tables, charts and so on. Learners *need* to know whether they have to be able to reproduce the

information concerned, or simply pick out trends, or recognize it next time – and so on.

Textbooks rarely help the reader regarding whether the visual information is to be learned, or understood, or merely noted in passing. By default, most just gets noted in passing.

Manageable chunks

Good open learning materials take into account the fact that concentration spans are limited. Material is broken down into manageable sections, each with a start, a middle and an end.

Textbooks tend to present large amounts of material at a time – the author continues until he or she has said all that can be said about each topic.

Study skills advice

In the best open learning materials, there are frequent tips for learners, regarding how best to get to grips with the various ideas, concepts and information.

With textbooks, how the reader learns is not usually seen as the author's concern. Readers are left to their own resources regarding the development of their study skills.

Summaries and reviews

With open learning materials, each chunk ends with some sort of summary or review. The review may well be made an active event – for example by presenting learners with a checklist so that they can test out how well they've got on with the material.

Textbooks often have summaries or reviews, but usually only at the end of rather long instalments of material. Textbook review sections are rarely turned into an activity for readers.

How am I doing?

Open learning materials try to answer this question continuously. Self-assessment questions and responses help to do this, so do objectives, reviews and summaries. The learner is not left long in doubt.

Most textbooks give little help to the reader who wants to know 'how am I doing?'

Feedback and modification

It is usual for open learning materials to be piloted quite extensively. Feedback is gathered from the learners themselves, via questionnaires, interviews and so on. Modifications are made whenever snags are encountered.

The only feedback many a textbook author gets is from academic peers – reviewers or referees. The average reader's views may not easily get back to the author. The exception is when a good textbook gets into third, fourth, fifth editions – but how many textbooks are that good?

Human back-up

Is usual to have some form of tutorial support for open learners. This may take

place in distance mode – or in face-to-face mode, or both. Open learners who have difficulties may depend on this support. Human support can even turn quite poor open learning materials into successful learning resources.
There may not be such support for the textbook reader who has difficulties.

Conclusions

The comparisons in this section are obviously prejudiced against the traditional sort of textbook. To defend this bias, I would like to remind you of two things:

1. *A textbook can indeed work splendidly if its user is skilled in the use of textbooks.*
2. *Many people who desperately need to extend or update their knowledge and skills are* not *experts in using textbooks.*

Therefore, the main principles underlying the best open learning materials are to make learning active, interesting, and humane – not to mention successful. Many of the principles mentioned above will be explored in detail in the next few chapters of this book.

III. Using Open Learning in Face-to-Face Courses

Section objectives

When you've explored this section you should:

- have some ideas regarding how open learning may fit in with 'conventional' courses
- be able to select the most appropriate topic areas for open learning.

Mix and match

Self study modules are the bread and butter of open learning programmes, but they can also be used to replace selected parts of conventional face-to-face courses, such as those run in colleges and training centres. Certain parts of the curriculum lend themselves best to translation to open learning form. It obviously takes time and energy to compose such open learning modules, though it may often be possible to adapt existing published materials for such purposes.

Where open learning material is being used to back up formal tuition, the quality of the modules doesn't need to aim for absolute perfection – the trainer or lecturer is still available to bridge gaps and help with problems. Even quite small elements of a course may be independently turned into open learning components – maybe in the form of handouts of no more than half a dozen pages or so. Certain hallmarks of open learning need to remain, however, to ensure effective learning:

- clear objectives
- plenty of activity
- self-assessment questions and feedback
- useful summaries.

Even the smallest open learning modules benefit from the use of white space for learners to write in as they study. The white space makes the module far more 'compelling' – it is then not just an ordinary handout, destined for filing!

The justification for the extra costs (financial or in terms of time writing modules) needs to be in terms of more effective learning, and the ultimate easing of the pressure on the teacher's time. There are several particular instances where it can be well worth the time or expense to add open learning components to face-to-face courses. I will describe some of these briefly under the following headings:

- Introductory material
- Much repeated lectures

- Remedial lectures
- Background material
- 'Need-to-know-before ...' material
- Bits you don't like teaching!
- 'Nice-to-know' versus 'need-to-know' material.

Introductory material

At the start of most courses, the first few sessions are taken up going over various things that the learners should know already. This is necessary to 'level' the knowledge base of the group in readiness for progress to more demanding material. However, all too often many of the group do not in fact already know the basic material. They may well have *studied* it before – even to the level of exam success – but how much of it do they remember months (or even years) later when starting their new courses?

So, in the first few sessions a class may consist of a diverse mixture of learners. There are those who actually know the basic material very well (and easily become bored and switched off). There are those who know very little of the basic material already (who may find the lecturer's pace too fast). The obvious solution is to provide learner-paced learning – self study or open learning.

An open learning module can be issued *instead* of the first few class sessions. Learners could be briefed along the following lines:

> *Come back in three weeks' time, having worked through the module I've given you. You'll need to make sure that you can achieve all the objectives in the module by then. The best way of doing this is by completing all the various activities in the module. It doesn't matter if it takes you two hours or two days – the main thing is that when you've completed the module you'll be exactly ready for our next session together.*

The slower learners can spend a bit of extra time to get to the starting point for the sessions to come. The fast learners (or those who know a lot already) can skim quickly through the open learning module, slowing down only when (or if) they come to something new to them.

An additional advantage of using open learning modules for going over fundamentals underpinning a course is that the modules make excellent revision aids. When exams approach, such modules make ideal revision tools.

Much repeated lectures

I'm thinking here about college-based courses where there may be some lectures common to a number of different classes or programmes. Have you got some lectures you always seem to be giving? It can of course get a bit boring giving the same lecture time and time again. If it gets boring to you, what may be happening to it as far as your learners are concerned?

If the total numbers of learners involved are quite large, it may well be worth the time and effort needed to turn such lectures into open learning components of their courses. A much repeated lecture is usually an important one anyway, so it is obviously useful for learners to have a ready-to-use revision aid for such parts of their courses. I'm not suggesting completely abandoning the face-to-face session, however. If the module is issued a little in advance of the lecture session, the live event can be used for discussion and questions, rather than merely note-taking by learners.

Remedial lectures

Even well into a course, it is often found that a significant proportion of a learner group has difficulty with some important aspect of the course. For example, many engineering lecturers find that learners are still lacking in essential mathematical skills.

The problem can of course be overcome by slotting in a remedial lecture now and then – but this leaves less time for the central subject material. Besides, not every learner will need the remedial lectures – for the more able learners these will be boring or even alienating.

If the problem is anticipated, open learning modules covering the remedial material can be issued to all learners in advance of the point where they need to have mastered the material involved. Even the slower learners then have the chance to practise and develop the skills concerned before they are needed in the context of the main subject.

Remedial help is usually most needed for the sort of topics that are hard to grasp first time round. An open learning module is a permanent revision aid – ideal for such material.

Background material

I'm not thinking now of the same thing as I described under 'Introductory material' earlier, though there is some overlap. More particularly, I'm thinking of those times when learners need to explore a topic *before* lectures focus in on the principal concepts or facts involved. Indeed, open learning modules are *not* the best way to cover wide ranging background material – the modules would take too long to prepare and to use. However, there are still ways of assisting learners to cover the necessary background work in open learning mode. A 'study guide' can be designed to channel their background preparation along productive lines. Such a study guide can refer out to various sources, but at the same time it can itself be made an *active* resource. It can use those mainstays of open learning: objectives, self-assessment questions and responses. Students are then in a much better position to *measure* the success of their background preparation.

What I'm saying is that you can prepare a useful open learning resource without much text, but with objectives, self-assessment questions, responses, and references. The text itself is often the least important part of the best open learning materials.

'Need-to-know-before' material

I'm thinking here particularly of laboratory and practical work. There is often a considerable delay before learners can be let loose on practical work – they need to have sufficient theory under their belts to make sense of practical work. This delay can result in unused laboratories and workshops for a few weeks, then hectic scheduling as all the learners come 'on-line' for practical work at once.

Suppose for the sake of argument that a class of 30 needed to prepare to be ready to embark on a set of five practical assignments at the first practical session. Suppose there were five short open learning modules available, each of which would give learners all they needed to be ready to start one of the five assignments. Better still, suppose learners were given a timetable showing which assignment they would do first, and so on during the first five practical sessions. Practical work could then be started much earlier. This would avoid the long, boring (from the learners' point of view) run-up where seemingly endless theory is being presented before the relief of practical work.

Bits you don't like teaching!
If you're a teacher or trainer, and if you're in a position of seniority, you can probably delegate such topics to someone else! If not, you're lumbered with them. Or are we really saying your learners are lumbered with you doing something you don't like?

This may not be the most honourable reason for spending some time and energy – once – and making an open learning module out of your non-favourite topics! But who will suffer?

'Nice-to-know' versus 'need-to-know' material
A formal lecture course may well need to concentrate on the 'need-to-know' material. However, some of the 'nice-to-know' material may be quite useful for your learners, so that they gain a fuller perspective of their subject materials. The problem is simple: there's always so much more 'nice-to-know' stuff than there is time to cover it. Reference out to textbooks and journals may not help the average learner – only the highly conscientious ones may follow up the references. However, if the learners' task can be a little more structured, they may take it more seriously. I'm suggesting the use of structured study-guide material, with in-built activities, objectives, and even self-assessed tests. A small duplicated 'workbook', full of white space for learners to record things in as they follow up references, is much more compelling and involving than a mere list of suggested reading. How many people actually follow-up 'suggested reading' lists anyway?

Which learners are particularly helped?

Let's look at those learners who benefit most from the use of open learning modules as part of college tuition.

- *High-fliers*. These benefit by being able to work at their own faster pace through open learning components of their courses. This is better than the situation they face in lectures, where they often get bored with the slower pace needed by many of their colleagues.

- *Low-fliers.* These benefit by being able to spend the extra time they need while working through open learning modules. They are then able to bring themselves up to the same level as the rest of their group for the start of further parts of their studies. Low-fliers may need to work through modules more than once – this is far easier than needing a repeat of a lecture! Low-fliers can put in that extra bit of effort without embarrassment – no-one need know that they've spent extra time. Of course, effort pays dividends – open learning modules can allow low-fliers to become higher-fliers!

- *Absent learners.* People who miss lectures through sickness or other circumstances may find it difficult to catch up. Copying down a colleague's lecture notes is a poor substitute for being present at a good lecture. Where an open learning module is being used, it is perfectly possible to catch up on it later.

- *Learners weak in language skills.* Here I'm particularly thinking of people learning in a second language. In lectures, such learners may be spending much of their energy making sense of the words themselves, with little energy left to begin making sense of the ideas and concepts being taught. Self study modules allow such learners the extra time they need to master the meaning of words – they can use dictionaries at will.

- *Turned-off students!* The people I'm particularly thinking about are those who simply don't like being on the receiving end of formal teaching! Sometimes mature learners are prone to being turned off by the formal teaching-learning situation – they may feel out of place, or they may feel that their experience is being undervalued. There are no·such feelings attached to working through a good open learning module. Learners' self-esteem is maintained or increased as they work on their own.

- *Over-anxious learners.* These are the learners who are most hurt by being *seen* to have got something wrong – for example, when giving a wrong reply to a question posed to them during a lecture. With an open learning module, they can make mistakes in private. There's much less loss of self-esteem when no one else knows about one's mistakes.

Over-anxious learners are often the ones who take revision very seriously, and they are further helped by the fact that it's much easier to revise from an active open learning module than from a mere transcript of what occurred in a lecture.

Conclusions

As you've seen, most college learners can benefit from the use of open learning components. It may be quite impossible to introduce a wide range of open learning resource materials 'overnight', but the range of such materials can be gradually built up until a college course contains the most suitable mix of face-to-face and open learning. The main issue remains to save human skills for things that really *need* human skills, and use open learning for topics where learners can best get to grips with things at their own pace and in their own way.

In the next few chapters I'll explore some finer details of what makes open learning 'tick', and how to go about creating new materials – or improving old ones.

2. Making Objectives Useful to Open Learners

Aim

This chapter aims to help you explore the role of behavioural objectives in open learning materials. I would also like to help you to make such objectives in material you write positively *useful* to your learners. If you're using materials which already have stated objectives, you may find that you can improve them considerably.

Objectives

When you've read this chapter, you should be better able to:

- Distinguish between aims and objectives
- Write clear, precise objectives
- Formulate objectives which are directly useful to open learners
- Allow objectives to play a major role in open learning materials.

What is an 'aim'?

I've got to admit to some cynicism regarding 'aims'! You'll no doubt have seen aims adorning many an objective-based syllabus. Such aims are usually followed by lists of 'sharper' objectives. The objectives are needed to spell out exactly what the aim means.

I sometimes think that the people who write aims in such a syllabus have the following definition in mind:

An aim is something you write near the top of a syllabus, which no one can prove your students haven't achieved.

So what *is* an aim? I'd settle for either or both of two descriptions:

- a broad statement of intent
- a 'flavour-statement', giving some ideas of what's to come.

It's not really possible to return to an aim, and use it to test out whether the learning has been successful. We need 'sharper' tools for this purpose.

Have a look again at the aim I started this chapter with. Do you notice that it's really quite broad, and doesn't give you much help about exactly what will be involved in achieving it?

What is an 'objective'?

It's a sharper, more precise statement of intent. An objective (in learning materials) is usually a statement along the following lines – with several 'completions':

When you've completed this module, you should be able to:

- sketch a grommit
- list the three main requirements for an effective grommit
- explain why grommits can't be used alongside an electric gubbins.

There are many ways of introducing the things that the learners should expect to achieve. Alternative introductory phrases include:

When you've worked through this section, you'll be able to ...
When you've completed this package, you'll be able to answer each of the following questions ...

However, I've also seen materials which begin with a statement like:

The expected learning outcome of this module is that the student will be able to ...

This sort of objective-writing is obviously *not* addressed to the learner; it's more like something to tell the trainers or teachers what their learners should become able to accomplish. This sort of statement of objectives is quite unfriendly and remote if read by learners themselves, so I'd recommend sticking to the more personal and involving kind of objectives, such as my earlier examples.

Objectives jargon? Have you met some of the jargon associated with behavioural objectives?

Let's look at some of the words which *some* educationalists like to use to classify and categorize objectives. They talk of three overlapping 'domains':

Cognitive	(knowledge, thinking, and so on)
Affective	(feelings, attitudes, and so on)
Psychomotor	(practical skills, and so on)

Within the 'domains' they refer to hierarchies:

Cognitive:
  knowledge
  comprehension
  application
  analysis
  synthesis
  evaluation

Affective:
  receiving
  responding
  valuing
  organization
  characterization

Then they talk of 'taxonomies' of objectives. But don't worry if you don't know or understand these terms; I think they are simply jargon which tends to get in the way. One problem is that the various categories overlap so much. Another is that words like 'analysis' and 'synthesis' mean different things to different people. If an objective is to serve a useful purpose, its meaning should be clear to ANYONE and beyond dispute.

In this chapter, I'm putting the jargon on one side, and concentrating on some down-to-earth criteria for making objectives as useful as possible to learners. (They don't need – or want – to know which domain or hierarchy an objective lies in.)

If you glance back at the objectives I started this chapter with, I hope you'll see that they are more specific than the aim. It's easier to tell from the objectives exactly what's involved. In fact, the term 'specific objectives' is quite commonly used. I hope you'll also find the objectives of this chapter meaningful and relevant to your purposes in using this book.

How specific?

One way of thinking about aims and objectives is as statements of intent with different 'specificity'. In other words, an aim is not at all specific, and an objective is much more specific. We could imagine a continuum of specificity (figure 1) – with aims taking up positions on the left, and sharp objectives on the right.

AIMS	OBJECTIVES
broad	narrow
general	specific
A few ...	... a lot

Figure 1 Continuum of specificity

(You will forgive me introducing my own bit of jargon – 'continuum of specificity' – to show how questionable the 'hierarchy/taxonomy' jargon is!)

In practice, we may not want to make the objectives as sharp as they possibly could be – there may turn out to be far too many of them. So a compromise may be reached, with objectives *towards* the right-hand side of our continuum.

We've seen that an objective is some kind of statement of the 'learning outcome' that is intended. This is sometimes referred to as the 'performance'.

It's possible to make objectives even clearer by referring to the 'conditions' under which the performance is to be achieved. So phrases such as the following may be slipped into objectives when necessary:

... under exam conditions ...
... using your textbooks ...
... in laboratory conditions ...
... working as part of a team ...
... using a digital voltmeter ...

A final dimension can be added. The 'standard' of performance may sometimes need to be spelled out. So phrases such as these could be used:

... to four decimal places ...
... at least eight correct out of ten ...
... in 30 minutes or less ...
... in around 500 words ...

However, if all the conditions and standards were spelled out in every single objective, it would get longwinded and boring for learners. I suggest including information about conditions and standards only when the learners *need to know* such information.

I hope that you're now beginning to feel that all the jargon we've mentioned is rather unimportant. The main thing is for your learners to know exactly what you mean each time they see an objective.

Whose objectives should they be?

The learner's, of course!

Objectives should be used so as to be as meaningful and helpful as possible to each learner. I make the point because so often we see sets of objectives that seem designed to help anyone but the learner! Let's look briefly at the objectives of some of the other people involved.

Syllabus-designers' objectives: Some objectives seem to be simply ways in which syllabus designers have broken down the content of each topic. Fine, if such objectives manage to help the learner too, of course. But the danger is that such objectives are usually written in language that the learner hasn't yet learned about – and this can be very intimidating.

Teachers' objectives: Breaking syllabus matter down into objectives can certainly help teachers structure their courses. But it's surprising how often the teachers don't let the learners in on the objectives! It's almost as if some teachers wish to keep the 'expected learning outcomes' secret from their learners – why?

Assessment objectives: A list of objectives can certainly be a useful frame of reference for structuring exams and tests. After all, the objectives should be spelling out exactly what the learners should be able to do. But again, the purpose of writing a set of objectives is not solely to make it easier to write tests and exams. It's much better if the *learners* can use the objectives too, to help them to prepare successfully for exams and tests.

The open learner may be doing much of the studying on his or her own. In conventional classes, a teacher often gives what amounts to objectives in informal asides – 'What I really want you to become able to do is ...'. This sort of objective is of course very useful. The isolated open learner needs this kind of help all the more. Let's explore in more detail some reasons for going to the trouble of writing objectives specially for open learners.

Why design objectives for open learners?

Listed below are half a dozen reasons for going to the trouble of making objectives directly useful to open learners.

1. *To show learners exactly what they're to do*
    - Alert them to challenges. If you write, for example, 'this one's a tricky one', learners will pull out all the stops to try and master it. If they're not alerted to the challenge, they may come to a dead stop when they find it's tricky.
    - Alert them to standards to be reached. Open learners may not be able to ask 'What exactly have I to do to pass?'; the objectives can make this quite clear to them.

- Alert them to *why* they're doing so-and-so. In 'live' classes, someone will ask 'Why do we need this?' The open learner needs to know this too – objectives can help to explain why various tasks are set and so on.

2. *To show learners what they've achieved*
   - Give them a frame of reference to measure their progress.
   Open learners don't want to have to wait till they're formally tested to find out what they can and can't do. A good set of objectives gives them the means to check for themselves how they're getting on.

3. *To show learners what they've yet to master*
   - when not yet successful, show them where the outstanding issues, problems or needs are.
   If they know exactly what the problem is, they're more than halfway towards solving it. The biggest danger is when learners have problems they *don't* know about. Objectives can help them see exactly what their problem areas are.

4. *To build their self-confidence*
   - allow them to see what they have already mastered. The feeling of having achieved the first few objectives successfully can be a big morale boost to open learners working on their own.
   - Let them see that progress is achieved a step at a time, even when the subject matter is demanding. A primary task may look formidable, but when it is split into a number of simpler steps, it becomes much more manageable. If objectives allow the open learners to see the smaller steps in advance, they're less likely to baulk as a difficult task comes along.

5. *To let them see why they're being asked to do things (such as self-assessment questions, activities, assignments, and so on)*
   - Objectives help show them the purposes of building in all the interactive elements common in good open learning materials.

6. *To allow the 'end-product' of the package to be measured*
   - Let the learners see just where they will be when they have completed the package.
   If they know where they're heading, they'll feel more at home all the way through their learning.
   - Let other people (for example employers) see whether the package measures up to the training needs of employees.
   People deciding whether or not to select a particular package look hard at the objectives.

All the above reasons for writing objectives are connected with the learners. However, there are other good reasons for using objectives.

How can objectives help writers?

Suppose you've already mapped out a series of learning objectives, before starting to put together a piece of open learning material. Here are some ways that the objectives may make your task easier, and your writing more rapid and efficient.

1. You'll be less likely to go off on tangents while writing text. The objectives are a useful reminder of what your learners need to achieve. Anything not directly connected with an objective is probably not needed by them – however much you're itching to write it.
2. The set of objectives provides the best possible framework for your design of self-assessment questions and activities. It's useful to try to cover each of the objectives with such learner activities.
3. If you're also going to design assignment questions (for example, for tutor-marked assignments), the objectives help you to keep firmly on target. They allow you to design assignments which test the whole of the content rather than isolated parts of it.
4. The hardest part of writing open learning material is simply getting started! If you've got a set of objectives, you don't have to start at the beginning. You can pick *any* of the objectives, and write a piece of text leading the learner towards achieving it, and SAQs and responses to give the learner practice at achieving it.

In Chapter 4, we'll explore in detail how best to move on from a set of objectives.

Mapping out objectives

What to include, and what not to include is the issue. Basically, it's a case of deciding what the learner *needs to know*. If there's an exam standard to be reached, that tells most of the detail about exactly what learners should be able to do at the end of their study.

There may well be many things that could be classified as *nice to know*. It may be worth including some of these things as objectives. However, if the learners are to make best use of your objectives, it's best that the objectives tell them very clearly the things they *need* to become able to do.

Making objectives useful to open learners

At last, you may be thinking, we're back to the title of this chapter! But by now, I hope you can see how we're aiming to make objectives useful to learners rather than merely useful to syllabus designers, teachers, examiners or open learning module writers.

If objectives aren't useful, what happens is that they're simply skimmed over

– or entirely ignored – by open learners. This does indeed happen with many existing learning materials. So, to make sure that your objectives are used, we need to make sure that they're intelligible, and serving purposes that your learners will find useful. Here are some general suggestions.

1. *Don't just list objectives.*
   Cross-reference them to self-assessment questions, text, assignment questions and so on. Let the learners know where they fit in. Printed asides such as 'This question gives you the chance to check how you're getting on regarding Objective (3) of this section' can be useful pointers to learners.
2. *Don't list too many at a time.*
   It's said that we only notice half a dozen things from a list, however long. It's best to introduce the objectives a few at a time. (Of course the whole lot can be listed as an appendix at the back of the module.
3. *Make them personal.*
   Write 'You'll learn ...' not 'The expected learning outcome is that the learner will ...' Learners working on their own prefer the informal approach. They need to feel involved.
   'You'll be able to ...' may even be preferable to 'you will be able to ...' Splitting hairs? To me the latter can sometimes imply 'we have ways of making you able to ...'
4. *Avoid unnecessary jargon.*
   If possible, avoid terms that your learners don't already know. A 'forbidding' phrase or term may stop learners from pressing on. Put things simply in the pre-section objectives, you can always list them rigorously at the end of the section, when the learner knows the jargon.
5. *Relate them to the experience of learners.*
   Don't keep objectives abstract. You can often add in brackets something like ('for example, you can ...') which helps your learners see exactly where the objective fits into their view of the subject.
6. *Make them specific enough.*
   Your learners need to be able to tell when they've achieved each objective. So rather than say 'List features of so-and-so', it could be more useful to say 'List half-a-dozen features of so-and-so'.
7. *Avoid vague words like 'know', and 'understand'.*
   Spell out the things the learners will be able to *do* when they 'understand' so-and-so. (You can get away with such words as 'know' and 'understand' in your list of aims, but they're not sharp enough for objectives.)
8. *Make them motivating and attractive.*
   Try to make the learners *want* to achieve them. Try to 'sell' the objectives to learners in terms of the *benefits* they will derive after achieving them. Even little additions such as 'This is a favourite exam question' can give learners extra incentive to master a particularly important objective.
9. *Point out to learners the important ones.*
   In a printed list of half a dozen objectives, they may all *look* of equal

stature. However, one of them may be crucial – others less so. A few words in brackets can tell learners about this. Otherwise, the danger with print or typescript remains that everything tends to look of equal importance.

10. *Mention the tough ones.*

If a particular objective is likely to be a hard one to achieve, let the learners know this. With advance notice, they'll try all the harder when they come to it. They'll avoid the pain of suddenly hitting something difficult. When already alerted to a challenge, most learners pull all the stops out and try their hardest.

11. *Return to the objectives.*

For example, at the end of a piece of material, review the objectives again. Remind your learners of the things they've been mastering. (Perhaps you'd like to take another look at the objectives at the start of this chapter? How are *you* getting on with them?)

12. *Make the objectives match assessment requirements.*

This is probably the most important of all the criteria I've suggested. When the learners have mastered your objectives as stated, they should *automatically* be able to do any exam question or assignment question correctly. Furthermore, they should *know* they can do so.

If they can't, it's the fault of the objectives writer, not the fault of the learners!

The suggestions I've made above may look rather demanding. However, the intention is that objectives should be a useful tool – particularly for your learners themselves. Let's summarize the main points we've explored in the form of a checklist – which you can now apply to objectives in open learning materials (whether designed by yourself or by others).

Checklist

Each objective should be:

- easily understood
- not too long
- unambiguous
- friendly and motivating
- not patronizing when simple
- not frightening when difficult
- clear and jargon-free
- linked to relevant sections of text
- related clearly to relevant learner activities
- such that learners can tell when they've achieved it.

The objectives as a whole should be:

- not presented too many at a time
- not like the average objectives-based syllabus
- all-embracing (covering *everything* the learner is expected to master)
- relevant (not including things the learner isn't expected to master)
- cross-referenced to text and the rest of the material
- importance-graded (ie the essential objectives distinguishable by the learners from the 'more-optional' ones)
- usable as a checklist when the learners have completed their studies of the material concerned.

Conclusions

Objectives are vital tools for showing your learners exactly what they're supposed to become able to do. In face-to-face teaching, students get all sorts of help regarding what they're supposed to be able to do. They ask questions, answer questions, listen to emphasis in tone of voice, and so on. Open learners miss out on many of these sources of help – and therefore need all the guidance that a good set of objectives can provide.

An important additional dimension for open learning objectives is the user-friendly one. That dimension is usually totally absent in the typical objectives-based syllabus.

When designing open learning objectives, it's useful to imagine a typical learner asking you the following questions:

- What exactly will I be able to do when I've finished this module?
- Which bits do I really need to master to pass?
- Are there any difficult bits I should be watching out for?

3. Composing Self-assessment Questions and Responses

Objectives

When you've worked through this chapter, you should be able to:

- accept that SAQs and responses (in one form or another) are at the heart of all high quality open learning materials.
- design SAQs which are clear, attractive, and above all useful learning experiences for your open learners.
- compose responses which perform a useful teaching function.

Perhaps the greatest need of open learners working on their own is that of knowing how they are getting on. Self-assessment questions (SAQs) are at the heart of any good open learning package; and, in particular, the responses learners receive when they've had a go at such questions have a vital role to play.

I should explain at once that there are several other names for what we're calling SAQs, for instance:

- DIY (do-it-yourself)
- ITQ (in-text questions)
- Check your progress
- Self-test.

All these things (at their best) are designed to achieve the same things on behalf of open learners as SAQs and responses.

In conventional courses, learners have regular feedback from tutors – and above all they can compare their progress with each others'. Open learners wish to find out how well (or otherwise) their studies are going before subjecting themselves to more formal judgements based on written assignments and tutor feedback – or before going in for exams. That's where SAQs come in.

What is a self-assessment question?

An SAQ asks the learner to *do* something. It may well ask the learners to recall something already learned from the materials or textbooks. But there are many sorts of SAQs, going far beyond mere recall. They can serve many purposes. Here are some of the kinds of activity SAQs require of learners:

- *making decisions*: for example, picking the correct option in multiple choice questions
- *application*: using things they have learned to solve problems
- *extending*: using what they already know, plus their thinking skills to go a bit further than the materials have already taken them
- *drawing or sketching*: for example, adding labels to diagrams
- *diagnosis*: for example, working out what is wrong or what is missing in some given information – textual or visual
- *guessing*: for example, having a go at working out why something happens.

These are just some of the things SAQs can do. But there's more to it than just *doing* something. When learners have finished having a go at an SAQ, they then turn to the *response* composed by the author. (In computer-based open learning systems, the response will usually appear on the monitor screen after learners have keyed in a choice of option, or an answer.) This is where the self-assessment comes in. Now they find out how right (or how wrong) their own efforts have been.

What do learners want to know?

Quite simply, learners who have attempted SAQs want to know the following:

- Was I right?
- If not, why not? What went wrong? What should I do about it?

What is the role of the SAQ response?

Suppose, for example, a learner has picked an option in a multiple choice question. The learner is either right or wrong. The learner then turns to the back of the module where the responses to SAQs are collected together. The response needs to be of value to learners who picked the right option or wrong options. To achieve this the response needs to do several things.

Responding to learners who choose the right option

Most learners appreciate a message of congratulation of some sort. Such as:

- Well done ...
- Excellent ...
- Good ...
- That's correct ...
- Splendid ...
- You're quite right ...

- Spot on! ...
- Bingo! ...
- Congratulations! ...
- Great! ...
- Right, of course! ...

The response next needs to remind learners exactly *what* they got right – reinforcement.

Responding to learners who choose an incorrect option

The response needs to give some sort of message of sympathy. Learners need to feel that it was a reasonable mistake to have made. They also need to know two further things:

- why the mistake may have been made
- what the correct answer is.

There are plenty of 'messages of sympathy' to choose from. Here are some examples:

- This was a tricky question.
- Most people find this hard at first.
- I used to get this wrong myself at first.
- Don't worry, you'll soon get used to this.
- I'm glad you picked the wrong option, because now I can explain to you exactly what to look out for in questions like this.

Since multiple choice questions are very versatile as SAQs, we'll look at them in detail later in this chapter.

If you're now beginning to think that the responses are actually more important than the questions themselves, well done – so do I! The responses reflect the things you would have said to your learners if you were looking over their shoulders as they got things right or made their mistakes.

One of the greatest advantages of open learning is that learners can make their mistakes in private. No one else need know they have made mistakes. They learn from mistakes they make, so that when it comes to 'public performance' such as tutor-maked assignments, tests or exams, the same old mistakes are much less likely. If there are lots of SAQs, learners can go back and try them time and time again over the weeks, until they build up both speed and confidence regarding getting the correct answers.

In the last chapter we looked at how valuable objectives can be to open learners. It's very important that SAQs are linked closely to these objectives. After all, the SAQs are asking learners to *do* the various things needed to achieve the objectives. Therefore, the learner who has achieved all the objectives should expect to get all the SAQs correct. More importantly, the learner who masters all the SAQs should automatically be able to achieve all the objectives. This also means that the learner who gets all your SAQs correct should also do well in any exams or assignments. If he or she doesn't it's probably the fault of your SAQs.

What purposes should SAQs and responses serve?

Before we start exploring various sorts of SAQ, I'd like you to think a bit more about the purposes that the questions – and particularly their responses – should serve. I list below some key purposes of SAQs.

1. *To give learners things to do*
   Merely reading can so easily be passive. SAQs involve thinking, making decisions, practising, calculating, and all sorts of other active processes.
2. *To show your learners what they have mastered*
   This helps to build their confidence, and shows them what is important in their studies.
3. *To show them what they haven't yet mastered*
   Once they know what the dangers are, they're in a much better position to get to grips with them.
4. *To catch things before they slip*
   It's all too easy to understand something one minute, and for it to be gone the next. SAQs give learners the chance to consolidate their learning before it 'escapes'. That extra few minutes spent reflecting on what has been learned is perhaps the most important stage in the learning process.
5. *To show learners what's important*
   If there are several SAQs about a particular thing, learners quickly catch on that they need to know that thing!
6. *To translate the objectives*
   SAQs spell out to the learners exactly what sorts of things they need to be able to do to achieve the objectives. In Chapter 2 we thought about 'conditions' and 'standards', and decided that it would be too cumbersome to spell these out for every objective. However, SAQs quickly alert learners to *exactly* what they need to do to achieve an objective.
7. *To develop learners' confidence*
   Many learners, working on their own, need to have their self-confidence increased. Getting most SAQs right has just that effect. So there's no harm slipping in an SAQ now and then which *everyone* should get right. Even when learners make mistakes with SAQs, responses can be helpful and encouraging.
8. *To give learners practice at responding*
   All sorts of assessment depend on being able to answer questions – often in writing. SAQs give learners practice – in private, where no one sees if they make mistakes.
9. *To prevent learners getting bored*

Working on one's own, if boredom sets in, it's all too easy for attention to wander. SAQs bring back learners' attention.

10. *To show learners 'where they're at'*
Open learners *want* to know how well – or how badly – they're doing. SAQs give them the chance to measure their progress – again, in private.

11. *To help learners choose the right pace*
If a learner is forging ahead quickly, *and* getting all the SAQs right, he or he can be confident that the fast pace is alright. If quite a few SAQs cause errors, the learner can tell that the pace needs to be reduced, and some revision is needed.

Quite a list, isn't it? This is because open learning (at its best) is highly learner-centred, and there's no better way of getting your learners involved than by asking them to do all sorts of things, and by using the responses to guide them.

How best can SAQs and responses serve their purposes?

Let's now move on to look at some general principles which can ensure that SAQs achieve their purposes.

1. *Early*. There's no need to wait until page 10 to pose the first SAQ. You can pose an SAQ even before you've told your learners anything! For example:
See if you can guess which of the following is the reason why so-and-so does such-and-such ...
This question wouldn't threaten the learners who don't know: you said 'guess'. Then, they find out from the responses anything they didn't know.

2. *Frequent*. A useful rule is to have an SAQ in view on each double-page spread. A double-page spread of pure text is very good at causing learners to shut the book!

3. *Not just recall*. You can get learners to predict, select, guess, calculate, apply, diagnose, draw, add labels, fill in blanks, and so on. There are plenty of things that don't involve looking back and merely re-reading what the correct answer is!

4. *Plenty of variety*: Use different types of SAQ every now and then: give your learners a change. (We'll explore several types briefly in this chapter.)

5. *Real learner errors*. There's not much point throwing in incorrect options which wouldn't be chosen by anyone.

6. *Responses, not just answers*. We'll explore this later in the chapter.

Types of SAQ

There are many types of SAQ. However, we can explore many of the uses of SAQs and responses by thinking about some of the following eight main types:

- multiple choice
- matching
- filling in blanks
- sequencing
- true-false
- completion
- fault finding
- open-ended.

I'll go into detail with the first of these – multiple choice questions. For the remaining types, I'll merely give a few guidelines, as the principles for multiple choice questions can easily be extended to most of the other types.

Finally, I'll prescribe a rather demanding list of criteria which you can use to measure the quality of the SAQs and responses in open learning materials.

Multiple choice questions

These consist of a *stem* (the bit at the beginning) and some options (usually four or five – but it doesn't really matter how many). One of the options, called the *key*, is either absolutely correct, or the best of the options. The incorrect options in multiple choice questions are sometimes called 'distractors', but, as we'll see, this isn't really appropriate for self-assessment question purposes. The incorrect options are not there simply to distract learners – they're there to 'catch' learners who've made anticipated mistakes, so that useful teaching messages can be built into the responses to these options.

With any multiple choice question (self-assessment or exam) it's important that learners don't have unintentional clues as to the right and wrong options. It's surprisingly easy to give such clues accidentally. If *you* write such a question, you'll probably be the last person to spot any clues!

Here are some suggestions to help your questions and responses be as valuable as possible to your learners:

1. Keep the stem as clear and unambiguous as possible. This usually means keep it as short as practicable.
2. Make sure that learners know whether to pick *one* correct option, or the *best* option, or *more than one* correct option, and so on. You can have different sorts of multiple choice questions, but the learner needs to know what the task is in each case.
3. It's best to avoid the following sorts of stem:

   Which of the following is *not* an example of ...?
   Which of the following is an *incorrect* form of ...?
   Which of the following is the *exception* to the rule of ...?

   Even when capitals or italics are used to emphasize the 'negative' aspect of such questions, learners still tend to look for the thing that is 'right' or 'correct', rather than exceptions, errors and so on.

4. It may be a good idea from time to time to get your learners thinking about the incorrect options. You could brief them along the following lines:

> In each of the following questions, select the correct option, and also try to decide what is wrong with the other options. Then check the responses to all the options, and find out how right you are.

5. Make the incorrect options as *plausible* as you can. If there's a 'silly' option, it won't be serving any useful purpose.
6. Try to choose incorrect options which represent *likely learner errors*. Then, in your responses you can address each such likely error separately and directly. In other words, choose incorrect options where you can make the response have a useful teaching function.
7. Don't write the stem so that it ends with the indefinite article 'a' or 'an'. This obviously gives learners a clue, directing them to an answer which begins with, respectively, a consonant or a vowel.
8. Make the options of roughly equal length. If one is much longer than the rest, learners will probably think it must be the correct one.
9. Avoid using any 'leading' words from the stem in the key. For example, if the stem asks 'Which is the most useful form of ...?' take care that 'useful' (or a similar word) doesn't stray into the key.
10. Avoid one option being more 'qualified' by conditions than the others. An option that looks 'tighter' will usually seem more likely to be correct, although learners may not understand why.
11. Be careful with the following sorts of words:

usually	never
often	always
sometimes	all
seldom	none

Words from the left-hand list shouldn't be mixed with those from the right-hand list in a series of options. Any word from the left-hand list will seem much more probable than words from the right-hand list. This is because we can rarely be as definite as to say 'never', 'always' and so on – there's *always* an exception or two! Of course, you can use all the words in the left-hand list to make up a set of options – or indeed all the words from the right-hand list.

12. If you're using a series of multiple choice questions, make sure that options (a), (b), (c) and so on come up with roughly equal frequency as *keys*. If it's been a very long time since there was a (d), learners who are unsure will tend to go for (d)!
13. With a series of multiple choice questions, make sure that there isn't a

pattern. Suppose you met eight questions, and sorted out (correctly) the first seven as follows, what would you guess for question 8 if you didn't know the right answer?

1. (a)
2. (b)
3. (c)
4. (d)
5. (a)
6. (b)
7. (c)
8.   ?

Most people would guess (d). Again, this seems an obvious point, but in practice (especially in multiple-choice exams) it has caused problems.

So, you can see that it's a good deal more demanding to design a good multiple choice SAQ than a simple exam question. The main part of any SAQ is the response, and you can't respond to mere 'throw-away' incorrect options. Now let's explore in a bit more detail the business of composing useful responses to multiple choice questions (remembering that much of this will be relevant to responses to other kinds of SAQ too).

Responses to multiple choice SAQ

1. The learner wants to know straightaway whether the chosen option was right or not. You can do one or both of two things to help:

- Start the response with something like 'The correct answer is (c)'. Then go on to discuss each option in turn.
- At the very start of each response make it quite clear whether the option was correct or not. For example:

   A Not quite right: you may have thought that ...
   B That's correct: it's true that ...

2. Make sure that your responses to correct options don't get boring. As I said earlier, there are hundreds of 'messages of congratulation' to choose from, so don't say 'well done' every time.
3. If the learner picked an incorrect option, he or she needs:

   - *not* to feel a complete idiot
   - to know what the correct answer was
   - to know what went wrong in picking the incorrect option.

I mentioned earlier various ways of softening the blow for the learner who has just made a mistake, by using phrases like 'don't worry, you'll soon get used to this'.

4. Give some sort of reward to the learner who picks the correct option. I

don't just mean give some praise; I mean give a little extra information of some sort. For example: 'Very good. This also means that ...' This helps to ensure that learners feel it is worth checking the responses, even when they are sure they've picked the right option. (If they stop checking, they might not discover their mistakes, thinking they are right when they are not.)

5. Make sure that the learner is reminded of *what* was right or wrong. Learners may not be reading the question itself when they are looking at your response. They may have forgotten what the question was! So, remind them in the response. For example:

> Sorry, but density is in fact mass divided by volume. To have picked this option you must have thought it was volume divided by mass – don't worry, you'll be having plenty of practice at this later in the module.

Good responses to multiple choice questions are therefore very much more than '(B): No, (A) was correct'. Yet so often, this is all one finds in the response section.

I've discussed multiple choice questions and responses at some length. However, as I said, much of the advice given here applies equally to other types of SAQ.

Before leaving multiple choice entirely, I'd like to summarize the particular advantages that such questions can have as a self-assessment device.

Some advantages of multiple choice SAQs

Multiple choice questions are often regarded with suspicion in educational circles. They are thought to be unreliable in exams. But the reason for that is usually that the questions have not been adequately piloted before exam use. Reliable questions can indeed be designed.

While the use of multiple choice questions in exams may have its limitations, in *self-assessment* they are very useful. Let's explore some of their advantages in open learning materials.

1. You can respond individually, and directly, to different learners making different errors.
2. You can brief learners not just to pick out the correct option each time, but to find out what is wrong with each of the incorrect options. This can help learners take note of mistakes to steer clear of.
3. It's much easier to write responses to multiple choice questions than to open-ended questions. For example, if you asked the open-ended question:

> What are the three main causes of corrosion?

you wouldn't know what learners might write. All you could do is given an answer, not really a *response*. However, if you asked:

Which of the following options lists the three main causes of corrosion?

you could then respond about why each of the incorrect options *didn't* list the main causes of corrosion.

4. While multiple choice can easily be used as SAQs for options which are either right (key) or wrong (incorrect options), they are also very useful for 'shades of grey'. One can ask:

Which of the following do you think is the *best* reason for ...?

The responses to each option can then discuss any good points wrapped up in the incorrect options, as well as pointing out the arguments for the 'key' being the best choice.

Matching

Let's look at a very simple example:

SAQ
In the following lists, link each country to its capital:

France	**Oslo**
West Germany	**Brussels**
Belgium	**Bonn**
Norway	**Paris**

The response to such a question would start with the correct answers, and then comment on the main dangers to check up on. (The response would, of course, be separated from the question itself – for example, at the end of the section, chapter, or module.)

The response might read:

France	**Paris**
West Germany	**Bonn**
Belgium	**Brussels**
Norway	**Oslo**

Most people find the most difficult of these to remember is Bonn, the capital of West Germany. Berlin is better known.

However, once the learner has paired off the first three pairs, the last one is left over, 'redundant', and is therefore obvious. A way round this is to use some added distractors. The question could then become:

SAQ
In the following lists, link as many as possible of the countries to their capitals.

France	Oslo
West Germany	Brussels
Belgium	Bonn
Norway	Paris
Luxembourg	Berlin
Denmark	Stockholm

The response could then state the answer, with additional comments, such as:

Check that you didn't put Stockholm as the capital of Norway; Stockholm is the capital of Sweden. Also make sure that you didn't list Berlin as the capital of West Germany – the correct capital is now Bonn (Berlin used to be the capital of Germany before World War II).

'Matching' questions, can be quite useful even when the final pair to be matched is obvious; for example, when the fine differences between a set of similar things are to be learned. Matching each of the things to its exact definition is a useful way of drawing attention to the fact that similarities exist, and the differences need to be learned.

A criticism often levelled against matching questions (and many other structured or closed forms) is that the information is all there in the question; the learners don't have to recall things. In the defence of structured questions, I would argue:

1. 'Recall' is by no means the only thing we want learners to become able to do.
2. If most SAQs asked merely for recall, open learners would quickly get bored with the SAQs and skip them. A variety of structured questions helps to make learners' tasks more interesting and different.
3. In real life, being able to *handle* and *process* information is much more useful than merely being able to recall it from memory. Structured questions help learners develop their information handling and processing skills.

Filling in blanks

Here's a simple example from chemistry:

SAQ
Complete the following sentences, selecting appropriate words from the list given below.

When any _____ metal is added to dilute _____ acid, a very violent reaction occurs and _____ gas is produced – it will probably catch fire. If copper, a metal of the _____ type, is added to concentrated _____ acid, _____ gas is produced, which is _____.

nitrogen dioxide	transition	nitric
hydrogen	alkali	brown
oxygen	hydrochloric	colourless

RESPONSE
The correct answer is: ...

When any ALKALI metal is added to dilute HYDROCHLORIC acid, a very violent reaction occurs and HYDROGEN gas is produced – it will probably catch fire. If copper, a metal of the TRANSITION type, is added to concentrated NITRIC acid, NITROGEN DIOXIDE gas is produced, which is BROWN.

If you got this completely right – well done. Do check that you got the acids the correct way round. Copper doesn't react with hydrochloric acid – whether dilute or concentrated – this is because copper is below hydrogen in the reactivity series.

If you included 'oxygen' anywhere, beware. I can't think of any metal-acid reaction that produces oxygen.

You may have said 'colourless' instead of 'hydrogen' – you're quite right in fact – but the name of a reaction product is always more important than its colour. Better still, of course, to say 'hydrogen, which is colourless' – but I didn't leave you enough room!

As you've seen from my example, the response *includes* the correct answer, but should go quite a lot further. Learners who have made particular mistakes can be helped as directly as possible. At the same time, learners who have answered the question correctly should still find useful reinforcement in the response, helping to ensure that they continue to look at the responses, rather than simply pressing on through the learning material.

'Filling-in-blanks' questions can be made more open-ended by *not* providing a list of words to choose from – but of course this means that it isn't possible to respond directly to learners who insert a word you haven't dreamt of! You'll notice in my question I had a couple of extra words which were distractors.

Of course, this type of question need not be confined to words – numbers, symbols, labels on diagrams, key points on graphs, and so on can equally well be filled in.

Sequencing

This is a bit of a game for learners. Their task is to place each of several steps in the correct order or sequence. First, have a look at this *bad* example of the genre!

> **SAQ**
> **Re-arrange the following steps into the order in which you should do things when making bread:**
>
> (a)   take bread out of oven
> (b)   turn on oven
> (c)   turn off oven
> (d)   weigh out flour
> (e)   measure out yeast
> (f)   measure out water
> (g)   leave in a warm place
> (h)   knead the dough
> (i)   mix in the water
> (j)   add the yeast
> (k)   add the flour
> (l)   take a bowl
> (m)   take out of oven
> (n)   put into oven

I'm sure you can see what's wrong with this? Firstly, far too many steps. How many learners would actually check their order against that given in the response? Secondly, of course, there is not *one* correct order in this example. You could make bread by a number of routes containing the listed steps.

So, it's worth adopting a couple of rules for sequencing SAQs.

- Make sure that there is one – and only one – correct order of steps.
- Don't use more than five or six steps at the most.

Otherwise, it is difficult to write the response. The response must, of course, include the right answer, but it also needs to explain the most likely errors. If we were to take on board all possible combinations of even five steps, the response would be far too long! That's why responses to sequencing questions should only address the *most likely* errors.

There is a way out of the difficulties of responding to sequencing SAQs. Four or five different sequences can be made the options in a multiple choice question! Then it's possible to reply about exactly what's wrong with each of the incorrect sequences. However, learners may well find the different sort of activity involved in sequencing questions can be a welcome change from option picking.

True-false

I'm not too keen on true-false questions in general. After all, the guess-factor is 50 per cent.

However, true-false questions have some uses. Suppose, for example, an exact definition is to be learned. A true-false question could pose either the correct definition, or one with a deliberate error or omission. The response to the SAQ could then deal directly with the error or omission.

When using true-false questions we need to be particularly careful that 'true' statements are absolutely true. This is sometimes more difficult than it seems! There are so often exceptions to seemingly true statements. We don't want high-fliers to choose the 'false' option because they happen to know an exception to something which was intended to be seen as a 'true' statement.

Completion questions

In fact, this is really just a special case of the 'filling in blanks' type we looked at earlier. Such questions are quite useful in little sets to help test-out several related bits of information. Distractors can be used to reduce 'redundancy'. Of course, such questions could be used without a list of words or terms to choose from, but then it would not be possible to respond directly to what the learner may have put.

Here's a simple example.

SAQ
Complete each sentence with the correct term from the list given:

- **(a) Current is measured in ...**
- **(b) Potential difference is measured in ...**
- **(c) Resistance is measured in ...**
- **(d) Current multiplied by resistance would have the dimensions of ...**
- **(e) Current multiplied by voltage would have the dimensions of ...**

> **watts**
> **ohms**
> **amps**
> **volts**
> **joules**

Responses to such questions need to give the correct answer, and some additional comment directed towards learners who make the most likely mistakes. Let's go on to the response to that question above – you may wish to try the question before looking at the response.

RESPONSE
(a) **Current is measured in AMPS. (Careful not to say JOULES here, amps are actually JOULES multiplied by SECONDS.)**
(b) **Potential difference is measured in VOLTS. (Of course there wouldn't have been any problem if I'd asked what VOLTAGE was measured in! Potential difference is the same thing.)**
(c) **Resistance is measured in OHMS. (Right now, what is OHM'S LAW?)**
(d) **Current multiplied by resistance would have the dimensions of VOLTS. (If you got this one wrong, it's OHM'S LAW that you need to polish up on.)**
(e) **Current multiplied by voltage would have the dimensions of WATTS. (It's easier to remember this by thinking of the name IVY WATTS – I × V = WATTS.)**

If you got all five correct, splendid. If not, have another go at this question tomorrow – and the next day – until you always get them all correct. Getting these dimensions right is very useful for our next section.

Fault finding

This sort of question lends itself particularly well to visual information. It also tends to be a rather attractive thing for learners to do as a change now and then. Such questions give some information, with in-built errors, and ask learners to spot these errors.

This technique can be used for all sorts of visual information, for example:

- diagrams (missing bits, extra bits)
- circuit diagrams (wrong components and so on)
- flowcharts (incorrect sequences and so on)
- maps (wrong locations, features)
- pictures (safety hazards, for example).

The briefing is important. For example:

What's wrong with this circuit diagram?

isn't as good as

This circuit wouldn't work: see if you can find three things you would need to alter to get it working.

Responses can give the correct answer, and a short discussion of each of the faults. It's also useful to mention in the response any correct things that learners may have interpreted as faults.

Fault finding questions can also be used with pure text, but it somehow isn't as much fun as with visual information.

Open-ended SAQS

All the types of SAQ we've explored so far have been 'closed' to some extent. In other words, there has been some imposed structure, with restrictions on the possible answers. This is excellent in allowing us to *respond* to particular learner mistakes. However, in many disciplines, learners may be heading towards formal exams with open-ended questions. It's easy enough to write open-ended questions. It's even relatively easy to design marking schemes for open-ended exam questions, so that all candidates are fairly assessed. (We'll explore the design of marking schemes in Chapter 6.)

When considering open-ended questions as SAQs, the real issue is how to *respond* to whatever learners may do. The problem is that we don't really know what the learners may have included in their answers.

It's quite easy to write a model answer, and use that as part of the response. But that's not really enough. The learners need to know *how* right or *how* wrong parts of their answers were. They may also want to know what their answers would have scored in an exam. Open learners need all the help we can give them about exactly how well – or badly – they are doing. If using open-ended SAQs, how can we tell them?

One way is to provide a skeleton model answer *with marking scheme*. Each learner can then go carefully through his or her own answer, finding out just how right or how wrong it was. Of course, the marking scheme needs to be a good one – one which caters for all reasonable alternatives that learners may have come up with.

Another way may be a cop-out – but can be very useful: turn the SAQ into a question in a tutor-marked assignment! It's worth thinking about this if the learners really do need a personal assessment and direct comment on their strengths and weaknesses. But then, of course, they no longer have the comfort of making their mistakes in private.

SAQ quality control

When I'm asked to judge the quality of open learning material, the first things I look at are the SAQs and, particularly, their responses. If all's well with these, the material is probably excellent.

Composing SAQs and responses is not just a job for authors of open learning materials. *Adding* new SAQs and responses, and *improving* existing ones are the most important aspects of modifying existing learning materials to turn them into resources which can be used in open learning.

I set out below a fairly stringent checklist regarding SAQs and responses. I'm not suggesting that every single SAQ and response should measure up to each of the criteria I list, but rather that *cumulatively* SAQs and responses should live up to the set of criteria.

I've expressed each of my criteria in the form of a question; adjusting SAQs and responses so that there is a favourable answer to each of these questions is one way of refining the interactive components of open learning materials.

Checklist

1. *Is it really a self assessed question?* How easy is it for any learner to *quantitatively* assess his or her performance? Is the response clear enough to attract the learner to do this rigorously? (For example, if the question involved a calculation containing several successive steps, can any learners who end up with the wrong final answer discover how much credit they deserve for those steps which they did correctly?)

2. *How useful are the responses?* Do the responses deal with likely learner errors? Do they deal with *all* such errors? Do the responses address learners' needs to know: 'Was I right?' 'If not, why not?'

3. *Does the question involve 'redundancy'?* Are parts of the question automatically got right when other, easier, parts have been completed? Would the use of extra distractors reduce such redundancy? Or is the level of redundancy acceptable?

4. *Does the question actually test something important?* Does the question test the achievement of a reasonably important objective? (It's often all to easy to compose a brilliant SAQ about something trivial, and much harder to compose one about something crucial.)

5. *Does the response congratulate (where appropriate) learners who got it correct?* Have you avoided being patroniziong in your praise? Are different ways of saying 'well done' used? And does the response remind learners *what* they got right – reinforcement?

6. *Does the response help learners who get the SAQ wrong to feel that their mistakes are reasonable?* Learners may feel that they have just failed something. Is this feeling dealt with humanely? Are learners given the feeling that it is *useful* for them to make mistakes in SAQs, so that they can discover the causes of such mistakes – and cure them?

7. *Does the response put learners who've made mistakes back on the right track?* It's of limited use saying 'read page 3 again'. Learners may make the same mistake again. It's much better to deal with the mistake head-on, in the response.

8. *Are both the question and response friendly in tone?* To make questions attractive and motivating, it's best to avoid formality. 'Consider ...' is more off-putting than 'Think about ...' (I've included more suggestions on user-friendly language in Chapter 5.)

9. *Is the task posed by the SAQ quite clear?* It's so easy for instructions to be ambiguous or confusing. When you look at *your* question, you see what you *meant* to ask. Will your learners read it the same way?

10. *Will learners be tempted to 'cheat' on the question?* Learners working on

their own can always choose to look straight to the response. However, this temptation can be reduced, for example, if the question is attractive and motivating. 'Cheating' can also occur if learners can see the answer to the question in the same 'eyeful' as the SAQ itself. The response should not be in sight while reading the question! Nor should the correct answer be clearly visible in text immediately preceding the question.

11. *Will learners be tempted to skip the question?* This is always a temptation – learners want to press on. However, if the responses are so good that learners become conditioned to being helped by them, the temptation to skip SAQs is reduced considerably.

12. *Does the question give the learner useful practice in things that may be involved later in formal assessment or exams?* Do the SAQs give learners that vital way of making any mistakes with the comfort of privacy?

13. *Have you avoided any sudden jump in standard between one SAQ and the next?* An unexpectedly hard SAQ can cause the learner to shut the book! Of course, if you say something like 'The next SAQ is quite a tough one; take your time with it" learners will accept your challenge.

14. *Are the responses really responses – or just answers?* Learners working on their own need *responses*, not just answers. They need a *response* to what they have *done* in answer to the question.

Conclusions

I've gone into considerable detail regarding the role of SAQs and responses, because these elements are the main advantage that good open learning materials have, compared to simple textbooks or manuals.

In open learning, it's the things that open learners *do* that are important – not just the things that they read.

When open learners have had a go at a task, they need feedback on what *they* have done – they need more than just correct answers.

Now that we've explored two of the principal dimensions of open learning materials (objectives and SAQs responses) we can move on to think about how best to go about the task of putting together a piece of open learning material in its entirety.

4. Strategies for Writing

My intention in this chapter is to help you organize the main parts of the task of writing open learning material. I'll also mention briefly the use of visual material, using non-print media, and presentation of material.

If you are more likely to be *adapting* existing materials, rather than composing new ones from scratch, I think you'll find the suggestions in this chapter equally helpful.

Objectives

When you've explored this chapter, you should feel more confident regarding:

- choosing an efficient systematic way of putting together the principal components of open learning material
- making sure that open learners can get the most out of any visual material you include (graphs, diagrams, tables, charts, pictures and so on)
- ensuring that any non-print media you employ are serving learners as effectively as possible
- using presentation or 'housestyle' aspects to enhance the learning experiences of users of open learning materials you develop.

Why do we need to think about strategies?

The open learning writer needs to be a Jack of many trades. It's not just a case of telling a story. The module needs to be something that causes learning to occur. It matters too *how* the learning occurs. The aim should be for it to occur efficiently, enjoyably, lastingly and actively.

My purpose in this chapter is to make it easier for you to organize and structure your tasks as you put together open learning material. Let me first try to scare you by pointing out just how many different considerations you're likely to be dealing with!

A good open learning module doesn't just contain printed pages which look more or less alike. It contains various tools to help the learning process to take place. The previous two chapters looked at some of these tools. The components in any good open learning module include most of the following:

- objectives (see Chapter 2)
- self-assessment questions (see Chapter 3)
- responses to SAQs (see Chapter 3)
- text (see Chapter 5)
- Introduction (see Chapter 5)
- reviews and summaries (see chapter 5)
- visual information (this chapter): diagrams, graphs, charts, tables, pictures, even cartoons perhaps
- Assignments (see Chapters 6, 7, and 9) for tutor or computer marking).

Other things you are likely to be involved with include:

- explanation of prerequisite knowledge/skills
- 'housestyle'
    page layout
    use of white space
    structure of the material
- signposting
    showing learners where they're heading
    showing learners when they've got there!

You may need to think carefully about exactly who the learners will be.

You may have additional complications, such as referred reading in textbooks, journals and so on.

There may be practical work to design and explain.

There may even be a home 'kit' to design and produce. There may also be components such as video tapes, audio tapes and other non-print media.

Once the material is beginning to take shape, you may need to assume an editor's role, looking at it objectiveloy and dispassionately (Chapter 12 may be useful then).

You'll also be involved in testing out your material, and making numerous adjustments to it in the light of experience – mainly the experience of your learners.

Now are you beginning to see that it's not going to be possible simply to sit down with pen and paper and start? It's unwise to start writing without a fair bit of planning first.

What comes first?

Let's restrict the argument – for the moment – to four of the main tasks involved:

- writing text
- designing self-assessment questions
- composing responses to SAQs
- writing objectives.

All these things obviously need to be done sooner or later. But the order in which they are done may depend on you. Different writers choose different ways of structuring their work. What works for one writer may not work for another. Let's see, however, whether there is a preferable order for these tasks.

Here are alternative strategies to consider:

Strategy A
1. Write text.
2. Write objectives.
3. Design SAQs.
4. Compose responses to SAQs.

Strategy B
1. Write objectives.
2. Design SAQs.
3. Compose responses to SAQs.
4. Write text.

What do you think? Let's turn this into a SAQ for you.

SAQ 1
See if you can decide why Strategy B is better than Strategy A! Jot down your main arguments, then compare them with mine in my response at the end of the chapter (p 74).

Let's now go on to have a closer look at Strategy A.

This way be the most instinctive way to work. But it has serious drawbacks. For example, SAQs and responses become 'add-ons'. They interrupt the flow of the text. Learners can simply skip the SAQs and responses altogether – the text will still make sense. Of course, we intend learners to *do* the SAQs – and *benefit* from the responses.

There's also the danger that, without an objective or two to keep us well-focused, our writing goes off at tangents. It's all too easy to write things which we think it would be nice for learners to know, instead of making sure that the things they really *need to know* are covered properly. Let's now return to Strategy B. I listed some of the advantages of this strategy in my response to SAQ 1. Let's take the discussion a little further now.

Strategy B has the advantage that the SAQs are not 'add-ons' – they are a *natural* part of the structure of the learning material. So are the responses. So the SAQs don't interrupt the text. Rather, the text leads up to each SAQ, then on from its response. So it's much less likely for learners to skip the SAQs. If they try to string together the bits of text alone, they'll find it 'jerky'.

Because, in Strategy B, some of the 'teaching' is done through the responses rather than in the text itself, learners find it *necessary* to try all the SAQs. This makes their learning much more active.

Avoiding 'blank-sheet-fright'

Every author experiences times when the words won't flow. Putting those first few words on to a blank sheet of paper is often the difficult bit. When writing an open learning module it's often hard to know just where to start. An adaptation of Strategy B can help:

Strategy B1

1. Write objectives.
1a. Pick an objective (not necessarily the first one).
2. Design an SAQ testing that objective.
3. Compose a response to the SAQ.
4. Write a bit of text to lead up to the SAQ.
5. Pick another objective – and so on.

So the author's task is made much more precise at each stage: thinking of questions, then responses, and finally the bit of text directly involved.

It doesn't matter much about the order in which the objectives are handled. It's possible to deal with each objective on a separate piece of paper, then gradually decide which is going to be the most sensible order of stringing the pieces together. The 'writing text' activity is turned into 'joining and welding' distinct learning activities into a coherent whole.

When should I design assignment material?

We've explored four of the main steps in putting open learning material together. However, as I remarked at the beginning of this chapter, there may be other important elements to think about too. If the open learning material is going to contain elements of formal assessment, the issue of 'assignment design' should not be left till later. Too often, assignment material, whether tutor-marked or computer-marked, gets added on after the open learning material has been written – and it shows! In Chapters 6 and 7 we'll explore the finer points of assignment design. For now, let's think of *when* to start designing them.

The best time to be composing assignment questions is at the same time as composing self-assessment questions and responses (with the learning objectives firmly on the table). If you do both at the same time, you'll benefit as follows:

1. Your material will be coherent, in that the SAQs and responses and the assignments will be testing the same objectives.

2. When you find something that's not easy to cover with SAQs and responses (because it needs a tutor's response rather than a standard one) this will be ideal for a tutor-marked assignment question.

In chapters 6 and 7 about assignment design, I also suggest piloting all assignment questions as early as possible – well before the material is printed! You'll learn many things from the piloting of just about any question – you'll almost certainly want to adjust the wording of the question when you see how learners interpret it!

It's also useful to design marking schemes and model answers at the same time as assignment questions.

When can I write some text?

Of course you *can* write it at any time, but I'm suggesting that various other things are best done first. The advantage of having things such as SAQs and responses already composed is that you know exactly where each element of text is leading from – and to. In other words, your task of text-writing is much better defined. So *which* bit of text is it best to start with?

Starting at the beginning?

The first bit of text is a very important one. It needs to have the right effect on learners. What should that first bit of text aim to do?

1. *Friendly*. If the initial text is formal or remote, learners may well feel that they aren't really going to be any more involved in the learning than they are with an ordinary textbook! So words such as 'you' (the learner) and 'I' (the author) are needed to start off in user-friendly manner.
2. *Motivating*. If the introduction is boring, learners may well close the module without ever getting started! If the introduction is stimulating, learners are much more likely to press on and get involved.
3. *Short*. There's nothing more daunting to open learners than a double-page 'eyeful' of unbroken text! That *looks* like a lot of hard work. So it's best to make the introduction as short as possible, then get straight into some form of activity – for example, a SAQ. You don't have to wait until they've learned something to pose the first SAQ. You can ask something along these lines – even on page 1:

> What do you think the most likely causes of ... are? If you don't yet know – just have a guess for now. See if you can think of three – then we'll go on to explore the causes in detail.

The introduction

Try the following SAQ, and then check the response on p74.

SAQ 2
When do you think it's best to write the introduction?

   (a) **before writing the text of the section, and its SAQ and responses?**
   (b) **after the text has been written, but before writing the SAQs and responses?**
   (c) **after the text, SAQs and responses have been drafted out?**

Having looked at my response to SAQ 2, I hope you're now willing to save the task of writing your introduction till rather later in your work. Of course you can rough it out in advance, but it's well worth doing careful fine-tuning of the important first bit of text *after* you know exactly what's going to follow it.

By now you should be realizing that writing open learning material is not one big, complex task – rather it is a collection of a number of short, interconnected, *manageable* tasks. The individual tasks are in fact quite precise.

Reviews, summaries, checklists

The best open learning materials always remind the learner of just what has been learned. Simply repeating the main points is much better than just stopping at the end of a piece of material.

However, it's much better to make the review or summary something *active* for learners. That's where checklists can come into their own. In fact, it should be quite easy to write a checklist for any well designed piece of open learning material – the objectives should lie at the centre of such a checklist. For example:

Now that you've completed section Z, check that you feel confident to:
   (a) ...
   (b) ...

The main advantage of having a suitable review, summary or checklist is that you get the main ideas to go *one more time* through each learner's mind. Successful learning is very much to do with how many times something has been thought about. Reflection is a vital part of the learning process.

I'd like now to explore three other dimensions of writing open learning materials: visual material, choosing and using non-print media, and signposting. These may not be quite so central to writing strategy as some of the things we've already looked at, but they're all very important as far as your learners are concerned. And, in practice, the sooner you start thinking about all of these things, the easier it is to ensure that they all contribute effectively to the quality of the material you produce.

Visual material

One of the principal differences between a conventional textbook and good open learning material is that the latter is more visually stimulating. However, it's not enough to have plenty of visual impact – the visual components need to be serving a purpose for the learner.

Visual components may include:

- diagrams
- charts
- tables of data
- graphs
- sketches
- photographs
- cartoons.

Let's work through a checklist of questions. It's worth having these questions at the back of your mind all the time you're putting together open learning material.

1. *Can I make it 'visual'?* An illustration, it is said, can be worth a thousand words! A good one certainly can save you time and trouble while writing. Or it can help make sure your learners get the right message from your words. Or it can show them an idea from another point of view.
2. *To what standard should it be drawn?* You may be no artist: that may not matter. For example, if you want your learners to become able to *sketch* a grommit, there's not much point having a cross-section of a grommit drawn by a professional graphics designer shown in your material. Your learners wouldn't identify with that. What they need is a *sketch*, and ours would probably be as good as anyone's.
3. *Do the learners know what to do with it?* Whatever kind of illustration you are using, you must be sure that your learners know what to do with it. They could, for instance, be expected to:

   - do nothing except notice it in passing
   - sketch it
   - reproduce it exactly
   - remember all the numbers in a table
   - pick out the trends (but not remember numbers)
   - interpret it
   - recognize it again next time seen
   - be able to write labels on a similar diagram

It only takes a few words of guidance to make the learners' task clear. Those few words can save learners trying to learn things you don't intend them to learn and make sure they do learn what you want them to learn. A few words in brackets after the caption may be sufficient, for example:

(You only need to be able to pick out the trends – don't try to learn the numbers.)
(You need to be able to sketch graphs like Fig. 3.)
(This diagram is simply to show you how a grommit is linked to the other parts of the dobulator.)
(You could be asked to draw and label a cross-section like Fig. 5.)
(Don't worry, you don't have to draw one of these!)

Choosing and using non-print media

Many open learning packages consist of printed materials and nothing else. We've already seen in this book ways that the printed material is not presented in the style of a textbook. The heart of open learning is the interaction between the learner working alone and the material.

Of course, it is possible to design open learning materials using media other than print, such as:

- video tape
- audio tape
- tape/slide
- computer-based material
- interactive video
- interactive audio
- practical kits

and various combinations of such media.

It is not my purpose here to go through all the pros and cons of each of these media. Nor is it my purpose to suggest to you which of these it may be best for you to use. However, I would like to arm you with a critical checklist to help you make appropriate choices. Above all, I'd like to help you make sure that any non-print media you decide to use are employed *actively* rather than as optional add-on material.

The checklist should be equally useful if you're thinking about designing some media-based support for existing learning materials, or examining the effectiveness of existing media-backed open learning materials, with a view to making improvements where necessary.

Checklist for medium 'X'

Let's suppose you've decided to use medium X (which can be anything from interactive video to simple audio tapes).

1. *Why is X better than print alone?* There should be good answers to justify using X. For example, video can be justified where learners *need to see things moving*.
2. *What will learners do with X?* If a 15-minute video is to be used, it's not much good if learners just sit back and watch the video. We all forget most of what we see on a television screen. Your learners need to have definite things to be got out of watching the video.

   For example, learners could have five questions to answer while watching the video. If such questions are already planted firmly in their minds before starting to view the video, the viewing becomes much more active.

   Alternatively, learners could be asked to answer certain questions after watching the video – to show them whether the important parts of the message have got across.
3. *What objectives does X cover?* It's all too easy to get carried away and stray on to matters that aren't included in the original objectives of the open learning material.

   Having made sure that the material in medium X does relate to the learning objectives, it's necessary to explain to learners exactly which objectives are involved. In other words, learners need to know exactly what X is helping them to achieve.
4. *Produce X from scratch – or adapt?* Particularly with video, the time and expertise needed to produce new material from scratch are usually underestimated. One problem is that we are all used to a very high standard of visual presentation on television. This means that as soon as we see something that is (even slightly) amateurish, we switch off from the message.

   It's often possible to start with material of high quality which already exists. It may be necessary to edit, selecting those parts which are directly relevant to the learning objectives, and cutting out things that are tangential. It will be necessary to negotiate with the owner of the existing material, but this is often much easier than you may think.
5. *How easy will it be for the learner to use X?* With audio tape, for example, we can safely assume that just about every learner has easy access to some form of playback. In fact, if audio tapes are a central part of your learning package, it may be worth including the price of a personal stereo in the overall cost of the package. Alternatively, it may be possible to hire out suitable playback equipment on request.

   With video, on the other hand, only about one person in three presently has access to playback at home. (And access isn't always easy – the rest of the family may have priority demands!)

Also, if learners are working on the material well away from video playback facilities, it's not very satisfactory for them to have to stop suddenly and be unable to proceed until they can get access to facilities. So it's necessary to flag – well in advance – when video playback will be needed.

6. *How early should I compose the X material?* Now we're getting back to basic strategy again. In fact, it's best to start work on any media components right from the outset. It's best to have explored the uses that you'll make of such media components right back at the 'objectives' stage of planning your material. However, I didn't bring this dimension in at the outset, for two reasons:

   (a) If you *start* with the media components, there's the danger that they'll take up all of your time, and the writing of the main part of the material may get very rushed!

   (b) When making audio tapes or video tapes, the first stage is usually a *writing* one in any case – you've got to have a good written script before you're in a position to generate good audio or visual material.

Signposting

It is beyond the scope of this chapter to go into all the aspects of style which have to be taken into account in designing open learning materials. Many such aspects are the responsibility of editors, publishers and printers rather than authors. However, the author can make valuable suggestions regarding the final appearance and structure of the learning materials.

One aspect should be of particular concern to you, the author, and that is 'signposting'. This is to do with helping the learners know where they're at, where they're going – and where they've come from! It's about helping them find their way backwards and forwards through the materials.

It's perfectly possible to add-on the signposting at a late stage in writing and production. However, there are advantages in authors being aware of some of the possibilities – even before putting pen to paper.

I'd like to list a number of things that you can do, to help your learners navigate their way through your materials. First, let's explore some things where you as an author are in complete control.

Author-controlled signposting

Words
Simple bits of explanation can be of great use to learners. For example:

Now that you've seen how ..., let's go on to have a look at the effects of ...

For this next part, you'll need to remember what we said about ..., and you'll also need your ... to hand.

We'll soon be exploring why ... happens. First, however, we need to think about ...

Flags

These are the small visual symbols used in many open learning materials to make various features stand out. Flags can be used for things like:

- prerequisites (things you should already know)
- objectives
- self-assessment questions (eg a large question-mark)
- responses to SAQs
- activities
- practical work
- pause time (eg a cup of coffee)
- stop and reflect
- review or summary
- key point
- suitable stopping place
- tutor-marked assignment (eg an envelope or pen).

But don't go overboard on flags. If there are more than about half a dozen symbols on a page, learners may soon get their meanings confused.

It may not be your job as an author to design the flags. However, there's nobody better at making sure that the flags get put in the right places.

Headings

Headings can be really helpful to open learners. Using plenty of headings helps break down the material into manageable chunks.

A glance through several headings on a double-page spread can alert the learner to what's to come. Question headings (you may have noticed I use these quite a lot!) can be particularly useful. Planting questions in the minds of learners creates a sort of thirst for the answers. This means that learners are then more receptive as they work through the materials. Question headings (like objectives) can play a useful role in alerting learners to what they should be trying to get out of the materials they study.

Numbers

All sorts of things need to be numbered, so that you can refer learners backwards and forwards through the materials. You'll often want to refer learners to *particular* SAQs, responses, diagrams, tables, activities, assignments, sections – and so on. So should headings and paragraphs be numbered too? Personally, I find a lot of numbering is off-putting and formal I don't like to see Section 1, sub-section 1.2, and sub-sub-section 1.2.4 and so on! You can often use headings instead of numbers. For example, you could ask learners to 'have another look at 'How a Grommit Works' on page 12'.

Objectives

Objectives serve many purposes (as you'll have seen from Chapter 2). They can help with signposting too. Where they're presented at the start of a section, they tell learners a good deal regarding what the section is going to be about. When objectives are listed towards the close of a section, they provide learners with a means of checking whether the learning has been successful.

Author-suggested signposting

Here, I'm thinking of other signposting features, which may be more the responsibility of the editor, graphics designer, publisher or printer, but on which you are in a very strong position to *advise*.

Boxing

Let's take an example. When your learners come to a self-assessment question, they need to know where it stops! Putting the SAQ in some sort of box is one way of making it quite clear where the SAQ starts and ends.

Boxes may also be used to make key points stand out. Boxes can also be used for activities, assignments and so on.

It's important not to cause confusion, however! Use different kinds of boxes for different things. Different thickness of line (or different colours) can make it easy for learners to recognize exactly what sort of information is in each box.

Typefaces

It's well worth authors knowing what typefaces are available to them, and making full use of the range. They may be able to use different sizes of type, bold type and a variety of styles including italic.

By using these carefully, it is easy to distinguish a main heading from a sub-heading and so on.

Print size and density can also provide ways of distinguishing 'need-to-know' material from 'nice-to-know' material. Important points can be made to stand out visually on the page.

A simple way for authors to let printers or publishers know what print size, density or font is intended is to use colour-coded underlines on draft material, with a key to explain which colour means what. But, of course, colours will be lost in any photocopying – so margin explanations may be safer!

Indenting

This is another simple, useful way of indicating a subsection or perhaps a SAQ. Like all signposting devices, indentation becomes annoying to learners if it is used in too complex a way. Have you come across documents where, at the sixth level of indentation, the line of print is only a few centimetres long?!

Colour

It costs a lot to use colours, unfortunately! However, if you've got different colours available to you, it's well worth making good use of them. For example, self-assessment questions could be printed in a different colour to mainstream text.

It's often possible to use *coloured paper* for things like SAQ responses, assignment sheets, glossaries and so on. This can make it easier for learners to locate them. Coloured paper may be quite inexpensive – much less than coloured printing. Whether or not you can easily use coloured pages does, however, depend on the way the material is to be bound.

Size of visuals

I'm thinking here about diagrams, sketches, graphs, charts and so on. The best size for these things depends on what you want learners to do with them. For example, if you want learners to become able to sketch something, it's not much good having a tiny diagram in the learning materials.

If you leave it to other people to decide on the size of visuals, you may be disappointed. They may be more concerned with fitting the various elements on the page than with the sense and structure of the material. It's well worth indicating to the designer, publisher or printer your intentions for each visual element in the material.

It's also useful for you, as the author, to state quite clearly *where* each visual should appear. For example, you'll often want certain bits of text to be *in sight* along with a diagram or chart. (It's very annoying to learners if they have to keep turning back or forward a page.)

White space

There are all sorts of uses for white space, including:

- space for learners to write in answers
- space for learners to make additional notes
- space to make important things stand out.

'White space' is one of the things that makes good open learning materials very different from traditional textbooks. Whenever your learners fill in words, numbers or sketches they are putting a little of themselves into the materials. This helps them gain some 'ownership' of the materials. Learners have a different sort of regard for materials they've written on. The materials become quite different from an ordinary source of reference.

How much space may be important. For example, if asked for a three-word answer to a question, learners would be very confused to be given half-a-page of white space to fill in! Or, if asked to sketch something, they'd be upset if there was only a tiny space to do so. So it's useful to indicate approximately how much space should be left in each case.

Page turns

Have you noticed how irritating it is if a major heading comes near the bottom of a right-hand page? It's equally irritating if a list is broken by a page turn. With learning materials, it's very helpful if each self-contained 'chunk' paragraph, SAQ, response, table, list and so on) can be seen in its entirety. Better still, if most pages begin with a heading or sub-heading; does it matter if the previous page had a little blank space at the bottom?

Conclusions

I hope you're not feeling like abandoning your intentions to write (or adapt) open learning material! I hope that this chapter has given you some thoughts about how best to set about the various tasks involved. You'll have gathered that it's very much a matter of concentrating on one thing at a time, but always with your eye on exactly how that bit is going to fit into the overall product, and how it's eventually going to look.

It's a good idea to get your hands on a range of different kinds of open learning material. Look at the different styles. Look for strengths – the things that make the materials work – and emulate them as you write your own material. Also look out for weaknesses in existing materials, and find ways of avoiding them in your own writing.

The real joy of writing open learning materials comes when you see your learners successfully learning from them. The challenge is not simply to communicate what you know. The challenge is to structure the materials so that learning from them is efficient, effective and enjoyable.

SAQ 1 (p 62) Response

I think Strategy B is better for the following reasons:

(a) Leaving text till later helps avoid running off on tangents!

(b) Writing SAQs straight after objectives helps keep the SAQs focused directly on the objectives. This helps to make sure that all the objectives are turned into activities for learners.

(c) Writing SAQ responses *before* text means that the responses can be real *responses*. You can explain things in the responses which may otherwise have had to go into the text. You can actually do some of the teaching through the responses.

(d) Writing the text last means that you don't risk writing too much – that may bore your learner! All you need write (at a time) is just enough to lead up the coming SAQ. Then a bit to lead on from the response of that SAQ up to the next SAQ – and so on. Your text passages then become 'bridges' leading from one SAQ's response to the next SAQ.

Did the arguments you wrote match some of those above? Please rejoin the text now, and we'll explore some further points about these strategies.

SAQ 2 (p 65) Response

(a) I disagree. The danger with writing an introduction before the rest of the section is that you may not quite know exactly what you're actually introducing. It's also very easy to get carried away – your introduction could turn out to be much too long.

(b) If you chose this option, I've obviously not convinced you that Strategy B has advantages over Strategy A. Please have another glance at the arguments I used.

(c) I agree. Writing the introduction last is much easier! For a start, you know by then exactly what you're introducing. This means your learners will get an introduction such that the section lives up to their expectations.

5. User-friendly Tone and Style

Objectives

By the end of this chapter, I hope you'll be convinced that:

1. Most learners find it easier to learn from materials which are written in an informal, user-friendly style.
2. Not many learners find user-friendly language patronizing – even though many academics, managers and 'authorities' find it beneath their dignity!
3. It's relatively easy deliberately to modify one's style when writing open learning material, so that it's informal and easy to follow.

Imagine you are writing open learning materials, or composing modifications (for example, additional SAQs and responses) to existing materials. Suppose you are considering what sort of tone to use in your writing. Many people now agree that an easy-to-read, informal tone is best – especially for learners who are working by themselves for much of their time. If you're already well practised in writing things in an easy-to-read, lively, informal style, then this chapter will hold few surprises for you.

Of course, not everyone agrees with the use of informal, friendly language. If you're one of these people, this chapter is aimed at you! Not everyone finds it easy to write that way – even if most of us do *speak* that way most of the time – even when teaching!

I quote here several things that people say about informal, user-friendly language – some approving and others critical – and I give my reaction to each point of view.

The arguments for and against

1. *Using informal, user-friendly language will help make open learners working on their own feel welcome and at ease.*
   I agree. Many open learners have sad memories of their earlier education. Many have felt patronized and insulted by teachers. Many have felt that

ego-trips were taken at their expense! Friendly simple language can make all the difference to winning their commitment. Friendly language compensates for much of the loneliness of the learner working alone.

2. *Using informal, user-friendly language will make it easier to learn – even with advanced subject material.*

    Yes, I agree. Advanced subjects may necessarily involve some complex terminology. That doesn't mean sentences have to be long. It doesn't mean the tone has to be remote and formal. You can write *about* complex things in a friendly, chatty style. That way the learner will think you're a friend and ally, not just a teacher.

3. *Using informal, user-friendly language will insult and patronize most learners.*

    I disagree. The only people who tend to be insulted by simple language in learning material seem to be academics! I believe this is evidence of elitism in our ranks! Do we wish to use language so as to *exclude* less able people?

4. *Using informal, user-friendly language will damage your credibility as an author or a teacher.*

    I disagree. If you were to publish a paper in an academic journal, informal language might cause surprise. However, writing self study materials is a very different business. In fact, it is likely to enhance your credibility in your subject if you are able to communicate it clearly and fluently. Using informal user-friendly language will enhance your credibility as a teacher. You'll still be able to use more sophisticated language in papers you submit to prestigious journals if you wish!

5. *Using informal, user-friendly language will extend learning opportunities to learners of limited language skills (eg students for whom English is a second language).*

    I agree. Many students have language problems – not just those learning in a second language. On average, teachers' language skills are more highly developed than those of learners'. Language should not be a hurdle. Unless it is a definite objective of your syllabus to develop your learners' language skills, you would do better to concentrate on the *real* objectives of teaching the subject.

6. *Using informal, user-friendly language will help your learners to become better at communicating in writing.*

    I agree. Many open learners need to develop their written communication skills. The more clearly they can express themselves, the better they will do in exams. They learn language from example. If learning materials are 'stiff and starchy', then learners' writing styles are likely to be the same. When learning materials are clear and simple in tone, learners are more likely to become able to express themselves easily and fluently.

7. *Using informal, user-friendly language will cause your learners to develop bad habits in their use of language.*

    I disagree. Informal, user-friendly writing doesn't have to be grammatically bad. It only needs to be simple. There's nothing wrong with short sentences. There's nothing wrong with using short words rather than long ones – provided the meaning is clear. There's nothing wrong with writing as one would speak – especially when communicating through teaching materials. Even the opponents of user-friendly style usually *talk* in an informal tone. If in doubt take a few recordings of yourself talking to people! The art of writing in an informal, user-friendly style is simply the art of writing as you would talk.

8. *Using informal user-friendly language will assist 'low-fliers' to concentrate on the topic, unhindered by the language.*
   I agree. 'Low-fliers' need to be thinking about the subject matter – not wasting energy sorting out the language as well. When learning from self study materials such learners don't have tone of voice to help them sort out the meaning of a sentence. The printed words need to communicate as clearly as they can.

9. *Using informal, user-friendly language will irritate high-fliers.*
   I don't think so. It seems in fact that even very capable students do not find user-friendly language annoying at all. Using simple language is not patronizing. If materials are easy to read, high-fliers simply read them rather faster. Freedom of pace is surely desirable in open learning.

10. *Using informal user-friendly language will allow high-fliers to learn even more rapidly.*
    This seems to be true. Simple language means that the high fliers can go through the materials all the more rapidly. They can forge ahead until they come to something that stretches them a little more.

11. *Using informal, user-friendly language is an art which I will not attempt to master!*
    If this is your decision, my advice would be to stay away from writing self-study materials! But why not master the art? It's not as if you will be unable thereafter to use more sophisticated language. If you master the art of user-friendly writing, it's another tool in your toolkit. You may be surprised at how often such a tool proves useful. You may even be tempted into journalism – where simple language is much respected!

12. *Using informal, user-friendly language will be a major aim of mine in writing self study materials.*
    Good. It's not as hard as it may seem at first. Keep sentences short. When a long word can be replaced by a short one, do so. Keep it friendly. Address your reader as 'you' – not 'the learner' or 'the student'. Refer to yourself – the author – as 'I'. Keep in mind the way you *talk* to students.

How can you MEASURE your tone and style?

One of the most frequently used (and abused!) devices for measuring readability is the Modified Fog Index. This has been widely criticized and it is indeed a blunt instrument. However, it is a start – and it most certainly can tell you things about the level at which you are writing.

The Modified Fog Index scores the 'reading age' of a piece of writing. If you score, say, 20, it means something like this:

1. People whose reading age is less than 20 will have considerable difficulties understanding your writing. They may have to read it several times before they get your meaning.
2. People with a reading age above 20 should be able to understand your writing more easily.

Calculating Modified Fog Index

So, how do you find your Modified Fog Index? Take a chunk of something you've written. Alternatively, take a chunk of something somebody else has written. Now go through the following operations.

1. Bracket off a sample of exactly 100 words. Sorry, this does mean counting them. Start at the beginning of a sentence, but don't worry if you end up in the middle of a sentence.
2. Underline each word that has three or more syllables. If such a word occurs several times, underline it each time. Then count the number of words you've underlined. This gives you 'L'.

$$L = \text{number of long words}$$

3. Count the number of sentences. Round it up or down to the nearest whole number.
4. Work out the average number of words per sentence, by dividing 100 by your number of sentences and rounding the answer up or down to the nearest whole number. This gives you 'A'.

$$A = \text{average words per sentence}$$

5. Add A to L.
6. Multiply (A + L) by 4.
7. Divide by 10.
8. Add 5.

The result is the 'reading age' of your chosen piece. Of course, if you're mathematically-minded, you'll prefer to use a formula rather than the list of steps above. The formula is:

$$\text{Reading age} = ((A + L) \times 4/10) + 5$$

How did you score? It's reckoned that a score of 20 or more means that the text is for the highly literate only!

If you're in doubt, try the test on newspaper stories. Even the more 'up-market' ones rarely score more than 15. Some tabloids communicate at under 10! Think what newspaper your learner would be most likely to read on a train – and measure its Modified Fog Index.

How can you get your Fog Index down?

I'm assuming you want it down! Of course, you may be thinking of applying for certain Civil Service senior posts where – it would seem – the thing to do is to use such complicated linquistic skills that only the highly educated and persistent reader can untangle the matrix of adjectival, adverbial and other clauses, yet still discover the subject, object and verb in each of your long, flowing sentences! Made my point? There are two simple ways of improving your readability – each bringing the Modified Fog Index down. A combination of both works best: use fewer long words; make sentences shorter.

I set out below some phrases which can often be replaced by a single word and some multi-syllable words which can often be replaced by a shorter one. Of course, I don't claim the substitution is perfect in all cases.

LONGER VERSION	*SHORTER VERSION*
establish a connection between	link
paying appropriate attention to	noting
in the immediate vicinity of	near
attain a consensus	agree
under no circumstances whatsoever	never
at every available opportunity	whenever
without the slightest reservation	definitely
arrive at the conclusion	conclude
reach the decision	decide
it may well turn out to be that	probably
with a fair degree of probability	probably
maintained in a perpendicular alignment	held upright
unable to proceed further	stuck
aligned in a horizontal position	lying flat
socially withdrawn and inhibited	shy
at the present moment in time	now
on a subsequent occasion	later
render assistance to	help
ascertain the exact location of	find
in a stationary state	stopped

LONGER WORD	*SHORTER WORD*
unprecedented	new
advantageous	useful
disadvantage	snag
commencement	start
consequently	so
deficiency	lack of
excessive	too much
inadequate	not enough

facilitate	help
subsequently	later
utilization	use
expenditure	cost
fundamental	basic
furthermore	and
illustrate	show
considerable	much

In the sort of sentences that have a series of items separated by commas, you can improve readability by setting the items out as a list, as is done often in this book.

If you did the Modified Fog Index calculation a little earlier, now's your chance to look back at the words you underlined. *Some* of them may have been quite necessary. But how many could you now replace with a word of one or two syllables? This can bring the Fog Index down – and the readability up.

'Action' language

Now I'd like you to think about writing in the first person and addressing your reader directly.

The traditional textbooks tends to rely on the third person passive tense. So it might write up an observation in the chemistry laboratory like this:

It was noticed that when copper nitrate was heated in a test-tube, brown fumes were evolved, which had an unpleasant smell.

But how much more involving this passage would be if it read like this:

If you take some copper nitrate, and heat it in a test-tube, you'll see brown fumes evolved, and you'll notice an unpleasant smell. Have you tried this yet?

Words like 'you', 'I' and 'we' make the reader feel involved. They make the writer seem more like a fellow human being. The question at the end of the above example is also there to make the learner more active. Questions make one think.

Conclusions

You've probably come to your own conclusions regarding tone and style by now. You'll have noticed that throughout this book I've been trying to write in the sort of informal style I'm advocating. I'm trying to give you a taste of what it feels like to work as an open learner.

6. Tutor-marked Assignments

There are all sorts of 'assignments' used with open learning programmes and in college courses where certain parts of a syllabus are covered by open learning provision. The most usual kind of assignment is the tutor-marked assignment (known by most learners as the TMA).

Objectives

When you've worked through this chapter, you should be better able to:

- list the main purposes which TMAs should serve
- use TMAs for those purposes
- design assignment questions which prepare your learners as productively as possible for their exams
- compose model answers and feedback comments to give learners maximum benefit
- devise marking schemes in such a way that learners can gain by familiarity with assessment criteria.

Assignments are at the sharp end of open learning. They are the milestones along the open learner's journey. They are an essential ingredient in preparing learners for formal exams, upon which their future careers depend. The first thing to come to mind when thinking about assignments is *assessment* – the score or the grade. But even more important is *feedback* which helps learners with their subject material, and allows them to gain from any mistakes they have made in their assignments.

Some tutors will be working at a distance, receiving material mailed by learners; tutor and learner may never meet, although telephone contact is often encouraged. Other tutors – those working on college-based courses – may know their learners; they may have taught them directly.

TMAs involve the learner's work being subjected to human judgement. The tutor will probably give a grade or score. More important, a good tutor will give feedback. Part of this feedback is helping learners over any difficulties shown up in the marked work. Just as important a part is giving praise where it is due, and helping to keep learners motivated and interested.

All sorts of questions can be used in TMAs: open ended questions (the most common form), structured questions – just about anything!

What purposes should assignments serve?

I would suggest that assignments can serve several purposes (which ones are most important will depend on the nature of the course):

- to help learners prepare for formal exams (where relevant)
- to give learners feedback comment on their work, and develop their self-confidence
- to give learners a measure of how successful (or otherwise) their work is (eg related to exam standards)
- to be a basis for communication between learners and their tutors
- to provide learners with deadlines and stages to help them structure the timing of their work
- to maintain and develop learners' motivation and commitment to their studies.

What are the tools in an assignment toolkit?

1. *Questions*. These may be open-ended or structured, depending on the nature of the assignment.
2. *Model answers*. These should preferably be composed by the author of the learning material (though they can of course be added by the tutor where not already provided by the author).
3. *Marking criteria*. These are devised by the author (or added or adjusted by the tutor).
4. *Feedback comments*. Comments on learners' work are written by the tutor. The author can, however, give tutors useful guidelines on this aspect, for example by writing a separate (short) 'tutor guide'.
5. *Assessment comments*. Comments relating to performance standards are written by tutors.

Feedback versus scores/grades

Let's first clarify what I mean by these three terms.

Feedback
I'm referring to the *comment* that learners receive about their work. Feedback needs to do a number of things for learners:

- *praise* and reward the learners who got an assignment question right. A mere tick – or a high score – does not do quite enough.
- *comfort* learners who got it wrong. 'Red crosses' can turn learners off for life! Learners who've made mistakes need to be reassured that the mistakes were *reasonable* ones to have made, and that it was in fact *useful* to have discovered the mistakes.
- *direct* learners who got things wrong how to get them right next time. They need to know how to have another go. They may need an extra question or two to prove to themselves that they can now do it.

Scores/grades

Here I'm referring to any kind of quantitative result. It may be a mark ranging from 0 to 10, or a percentage, or any other number. Or it may be a letter representing a grade.

There are many possible combinations of feedback and scores/grades. Let's think briefly about six of them.

1. *Purely feedback – no mention of scores.* This could be tutor feedback or computer-generated feedback (more about this in Chapter 7). The role of such feedback is to praise, comfort and direct – as explained above. Learners are able to tell from such feedback whether they have done brilliantly or otherwise. It may be kinder to learners who have done poorly not to have a score to show just *how* poorly they have done.
2. *Feedback with scores that are not important.* Feedback (as described above) can be accompanied by a quantitative measure of performance, with reassuring words like 'Don't take too much notice of your score – these are 'fun' scores at this stage, and don't count in your final grading.'
3. *Feedback, with scores that count.* This is self-explanatory. The scores will, of course, be taken more seriously by learners.
4. *Feedback, with detailed scoring breakdown.* Obviously, such scoring counts towards assessment. However, the detail in itself may be very useful to learners, allowing them to see exactly where they have gained or lost marks.
5. *Assessment record only.* This may be a printout of a learner's record of achievement. It may help the learner to see the general pattern of his or her progress over a number of assignments or tasks. It can also help tutors to identify the strengths and weaknesses of learners – and to give help accordingly.
6. *Assessment (or score) only.* The most obvious example is the exam result. Learners are informed of their scores, but don't get much (or any) feedback regarding what was correct and what wasn't.

What do learners look for first?

The score or grade! All learners getting back an assignment want to know straightaway how well (or badly) they have done. If the score is at the end of several pages, learners will thumb through quickly until they find it. I'd go as far as to suggest that the score can completely 'eclipse' the feedback!

Let's imagine three learners, Janet (a high-flier), John (an average learner) and Jim (he's struggling).

Janet's score is 85 per cent (or grade A). What does she do? She's quite likely to say to herself 'Great!' But is she likely to look carefully at the feedback? Will she check to see exactly where she lost the missing 15 per cent of her score? I think not. And who can blame her? She's done well. But the feedback may well have proved useful to her – even if she didn't need it very much.

John's score is 60 per cent (or grade C). He's passed – he's alright. Will he bother to look at the feedback in detail? He may well be relieved to have passed another assignment and he most concerned now to press on and try to pass the next one.

Jim failed! His score was 35 per cent (or grade E). What does he do? Does he carefully look through the marked work for all the comments that explain to him exactly what went wrong, and what to do next time? Or does he take one look at that score and tear up the assignment in disgust? I've watched that happen. However useful the feedback could have been, it was lost for ever.

What can we do about scores and feedback?

I've been trying to show that when learners get scores and feedback at the same instant, the scores may dominate at the expense of the feedback.

If it is necessary for score and feedback to reach learners at the same time, I think the best way out is to make it possible for them to check exactly how the score was arrived at – for example, by referring to a model answer and marking scheme.

But it might be better if the marked assignment reached learners with feedback comments *only*. Learners would go searching diligently through all the comments, trying to tell whether they had done well or not. So at least the feedback would be being used. The tutor could give the score a week or so later in a telephone discussion (or in a subsequent face-to-face session if such existed). The learners would have had the opportunity to benefit from the feedback without being distracted by the score.

I hope I've convinced you that learners (especially open-learners) will take any score or grade you give them very seriously. They're likely to feel that you're assessing *them*, not just their work. On the one hand, you may be obliged to make their scores realistic, to prepare them for the standard of some forthcoming exam. On the other hand, you need to try to prevent them being blinded to the feedback you give them. It's a dilemma sometimes! An important part of the solution is to make the scoring as 'open' as possible. Let your learners see exactly how their scores are arrived at. Let them learn from your scoring criteria – as well as from the feedback comments you provide.

Let's now go on to think in some detail about the optimum design of the most common sort of assignment – the TMA.

Design of tutor-marked assignments

I suggest below a checklist of criteria for the design of useful TMA questions. (It's rarely possible to fulfil all of these criteria in one's initial design, and ways of improving assignments during and after the piloting stage are discussed subsequently.)

1. *Is the question clear and unambiguous?* Will each learner int erpret it in the way it was intended to be read? More marks are lost in exams through misinterpretation of questions than from ignorance.
2. *Does the question directly relate to stated learning objectives?* How unfair it is for learners to be asked to do something that didn't seem to be on the agenda.
3. *Have learners been adequately prepared for the question (eg through self-assessment questions)?* I'm not suggesting that learners should already have done exactly the same questions in SAQs, but that the SAQs or other material should have helped them develop thes skills and knowledge that they need to answer the TMA questions.
4. *Are there several ways of answering the question properly?* This may be fine, but it does mean that alternative marking schemes may be needed for the variety of answers. It's usually easier in the long run to make the question so that there is only really one best way of tackling it.
5. *Does it prepare learners for the sort of question that may be met in formal assessments or exams?* Of course, the TMA may itself be a formal assessment! But if an exam is coming up later, the tutor feedback on exam-like questions can be most useful to learners.
6. *Is the main purpose of the question (for the learner) assessment or feedback?* If the main purpose is assessment, the marking scheme needs to be very watertight and polished. If the main purpose is feedback, the marks may well not count, and the tutor response can be oriented towards helping learners.
7. *If the assignment is to be used for assessment, can learners tell how many marks go with each question?*
   Learners are very good at matching effort to marks. If one thing carries ten marks and another carries only two, they know where to spend most of their time. It is useful to show learners:

   - how many marks go with each question – especially when some are worth more than others
   - how many marks go with the different parts of any longer questions.

8. *Will it be useful to prepare a model answer (or answers) to issue to learners along with feedback?*
   Model answers can make it quicker to give direct, appropriate feedback to each learner. Of course, it may happen that model answers get circulated between learners who know each other – but that doesn't happen as often as you might think.

9. *Does the assignment as a whole test the main things the learner needs?*
   It's all too easy for an assignment to test a particular part of what the learner needs to know – because that part happens to be easier to test.

10. *Does the assignment begin with fairly easy questions?* The most difficult stage in doing a TMA is very often getting started. Learners can be eased into the assignment by a few questions which are less demanding than those to come.

11. *Have 'either/or' choices been built in where appropriate (eg for learners with different needs or interests)?* Learning materials can be designed to serve a variety of learners with different needs, abilities and experience. The same tutor can give appropriate feedback to each sort of learner. Of course, this 'differentiation' is not possible if all the learners are aiming at the same examination standard.

TMAs are serious stuff

The average open learner takes TMAs – particularly the very first one – very seriously.

When learners send in a TMA, they are submitting themselves to the judgement of someone they perceive as an expert. It may be the first time for years that they have done this.

Imagine how you would feel as an open learner sending in your very first TMA. You don't yet know your tutor and you've not been assessed by a tutor or anybody else for years, perhaps since schooldays! You'd probably be experiencing a mixture of strong emotions and have lots of questions buzzing around in your head. Here are some of the things learners have told me they felt at the point of sending in their first TMA.

- apprehensive (most say this!)
- vulnerable
- exposed
- excited
- will he think I'm an idiot?
- it is good enough?
- when will I know how I've done?
- I hope she can read it!
- have I made a fool of myself?
- did I do enough?
- will he be gentle with me?

- why did I start this course?
- I'm glad that's over!
- When can I get on with section 2?
- Oh, blow it, I did my best!

Assignments are often a very emotional, (possibly painful) part of the open learning experience. So there's no place where we have to be more careful in our use of words, making sure we communicate clearly and unambiguously.

Designing a marking scheme

Designing a solid marking scheme is well worth the effort. Where a single tutor is marking all the assignments, it is tempting not to bother with marking schemes at all. But if you write a popular open learning module, your assignments will have to be marked by lots of other tutors. For other people to mark your assignments well, it's essential to have a marking scheme to indicate clearly how many marks are scored by each component or step. A good marking scheme will usually deal carefully with 'borderline' issues – what gets the mark, and what loses it.

A good marking scheme can also be a valuable instrument to share with learners. Learners can gain much valuable information about where credit is gained (or lost) through a marking scheme. I set out below a checklist of criteria to use in devising marking schemes.

1. *Could* anyone *mark any assignment and agree its score within a mark or two?* This may seem a formidable criterion – it is! But in many national exams teams of examiners have to be able to mark scripts to an accuracy of about one per cent.
2. *Does the scheme allow credit for alternative good answers?* If the TMA question is at all ambiguous, the scheme may need to cater for learners interpreting the question in different but equally correct ways. Even with a good TMA question, there are often alternative routes to the right answer, or alternative – but different – good answers. The marking scheme needs to allow for all reasonable alternatives, fairly.
3. *Does the scheme distribute marks fairly, according to the relative importance of different components of answers?* Ideally, the questions themselves will have made it clear to learners where the marks lie. The marking scheme needs, on the one hand, to be faithful to the question; but on the other hand it needs to give fair credit for everything learners have got correct. It also needs to give fair penalties for all mistakes.
4. *Does the scheme allow 'consequential' marks when an early mistake affects later parts of an answer?* This particularly applies to calculation-type questions. If a mistake is made early in an answer, but all subsequent steps are done correctly, a good marking scheme will give credit for each correct step *operation*, despite the fact that the final answer was wrong.

So, a learner could end up with 18 out of 20 marks, even for a wrong answer.

5. *Does the scheme make it quicker and easier to mark assignments?* I've often had on my desk a pile of 400 exam scripts. I've learned over the years that the first 50 will take about a third of the total time, and about half of the total sweat! Once the marking scheme is thoroughly learned and understood, each decision of 'to award or not to award' becomes much easier to make; marking speeds up greatly. Therefore, for anyone expecting to mark a fair number of assignments, even if over a long period of time, a good marking scheme soon pays for itself in terms of time saved.

6. *Is the standard of marking as close as possible to that of any formal tests or exams the learners may be preparing for?* It would be very sad if an open learner consistently got 80 per cent in TMAs, then failed a national exam. It's well worth using every trick in the trade to find out what the *real* marketing criteria are going to be. That may mean signing up as an examiner yourself!

7. *Does the marking scheme remove 'subjective' marking (scratching one's head, then putting down a number between 1 and 20 – perhaps the number one first thought of)?* It's terrible to treat learners' work so callously, but it does happen. Even from the tutor's point of view, surely it's more comfortable to know that the marking is objective and fair – to know that if you have a bad day tomorrow, your marking will still be as fair as it is today.

8. *Could the marking scheme be issued to learners, along with a model answer, to show them exactly how the assignment should best be tackled?* I've proved to my own satisfaction that my students have learned more from my marking schemes than from my lectures or handouts! The thing about a marking scheme is that students identify themselves closely with its use – they concentrate. They see from it what gains credit. And they see from it what *loses* marks: those mistakes they never make again!

9. *Could the marking scheme be issued to learners, for them to mark their own assignments?* This is a useful practice for early assignments, or 'dry-run' preparation for exams, when learners may benefit from being able to discover their mistakes in private.

10. *Could the marking scheme along with model answers be published in a future edition of the study material as an exemplar?* This is the real challenge. How many of us are prepared to put our assessment criteria up for public scrutiny? Even chief examiners of national examining boards are sometimes self-conscious about this. However, think of the boost to the credibility of open learning materials which did just this. Open learning is learner-centred – and this entails letting learners in on everything.

A demanding list of criteria, I think you'll agree. But a marking scheme is written once, then used many times. Of course, it will be modified according to experience gained while using it, and it will get better and better.

A marking scheme must not be an afterthought – something done in a rush at the last minute. The best time to design the marking scheme is at the time the questions themselves (and model answers) are being designed – with the learning objectives firmly in sight.

Improving assignments during piloting

If you write a complete open learning package, the assignments are the things you'll want to change first. Your open learning text may need minimal adjustments during piloting. Your SAQs and responses may only need the odd bit of clarification here and there. But TMAs are another matter! However good assignment questions are, they'll not be perfect at first.

Changes to help learners

You may want to make changes and adjustments to TMAs after the whole package has been printed. For this reason it is a good idea to have the assignments printed separately. The text in the module need simply say! 'Now please complete assignment no. 1 supplied separately and return it to your tutor.'

After the first 50 learners have worked through the assignments, you'll know where changes are needed in the questions:

- changes to stop learners running off on tangents
- changes to prevent learners from misinterpreting questions – even questions you thought were impossible to misinterpret
- changes of emphasis, to help learners identify what the real points of some of the questions are – even the odd underlining of a key word may make all the difference
- changes in length of assignment: feedback from learners often shows that what were intended to be 'equal' assignments turn out to be far from equal in practice.

Even *before* the open learning material is produced (or written) try out the assignment questions on a small pilot group of learners. If possible use some 'live' students – you can ask them things as well as analyse their work. Take notice of things most of them do well, and of common mistakes. The mistakes may well be your fault.

Changes to help tutors

It's a good idea to get a few different tutors to mark the first batches of assignments during piloting of open learning material. Better still to have some pilot learner assignments photocopied and marked by *each* of several tutors separately. If the marks agree more or less you may be justly proud of your hard work on the marking scheme.

In the light of the pilot experience, you'll want to make changes to the questions themselves:

- when learners find them too hard
- when learners find them too easy
- when misinterpretation often happens
- when tutors find them hard to mark fairly
- when there turn out to be serval ways of answering the question well.

You'll also want to make changes to the marking schemes:

- when allocating marks fairly proves difficult
- when agreement on the 'score' of a specimen assignment is hard to reach among several tutors
- when important parts of the answer need to carry more credit, so that learners see what's important.

Changes to enhance credibility

Here I'm thinking of changes which might be required, perhaps at a later stage, when looking at the learning material as a whole:

- fine-tuning questions and marking standards to those that the learners will face from external examining bodies and so on
- spreading credit more fairly over the course as a whole
- changes to reflect new perspectives or emphases as the subject itself develops.

Conclusions

I hope the above will have impressed you with the seriousness of TMA questions and marking schemes. Assignments are the 'sharp end' of open learning materials – at least in the eyes of the learners. Assignments are the way in which learners can prove themselves to themselves as well as to outsiders such as tutors. It matters a lot that they are given every chance to do themselves full justice.

7. Computer-marked Assignments

Objectives

By the end of this chapter, you should be able to:

- extend the principles of writing SAQs and responses outlined in Chapter 3 (particularly multiple choice format) to computer-marked assignments (CMAs) and feedback response elements
- include in the computer feedback suitable introductory and concluding paragraphs
- decide the optimum balance between feedback and assessment in your CMAs (in light of the discussion in Chapter 6).
- use CMA formats to gather information about learners' experiences of various aspects of their studies.

I'm assuming that you've looked in detail at certain earlier parts of this book. Before reading on, you may wish quickly to look back at a few topics which are important here:

- Chapter 3: SAQ and response design, particularly multiple choice questions
- Chapter 5: readability and 'action language' are directly relevant to the design of such feedback.
- Chapter 6: I went to some lengths trying to help you to think about open learners' feelings about being assessed by a tutor. Similar feelings are bound to exist regarding computer-based assessment. I'd like you particularly to continue to bear in mind the 'feedback versus scores/grades' discussion.

What is a computer-marked assignment?

A computer-marked assignment is one where learners' answers are processed by a computer. For this to happen, learners answers need to be relatively simple to process. The most common choice for such assignments is multiple choice questions. These usually involve four options – the learner chooses the one he or she thinks most likely to be correct. The learner then fills in the letter corresponding to the chosen option on a form or card. At the marking location the learner's responses will be keyed into the computer (or 'optically read'), and the computer will then process the choices in terms of which are correct and which aren't.

The story could end there – with the learner simply being sent a score. However, the computer can do much more than this – and very quickly. The computer can print out a *feedback* response to each of the learner's choices. In this way, the computer can 'reply' to each learner individually, depending on which questions were answered correctly or wrongly.

Of course, the computer doesn't design the responses! Human skills and experience are needed for that. The writer of each question is the best person to decide exactly what will be said to learners. Especially important is deciding exactly what message should reach the learner who picks a wrong option.

In Chapter 3 we explored quite fully the things to bear in mind when responding to learners' choices. Just a reminder about one key point: learners need a response to what *they* did – ie the option they chose. If it was wrong, they need to know *why* they made the mistake. So a typical response to a wrong choice of option would look something like this:

Question 5 You chose option (c). Sorry, but it wouldn't do to have a digital voltmeter with an input impedance of 10 ohms. Such a low impedance would effectively short out the circuit whose voltages you wished to measure. The best meters have input impedances of over 1 000 000 ohms (1 megaohm). When you chose '10 ohms' you were probably thinking of the conditions needed to measure *resistance* not voltage? Most of us confuse the two at first.

What bits make up a CMA?

We've mentioned the most important components of CMAs – questions and responses. A typical CMA may involve ten four-option multiple choice questions. That means, of course, that 40 responses need to be written. Since any learner will only see *one* response to each question, each of the responses needs to be self-sufficient. Writing the responses to a set of CMA qestions takes most of the time, and much of the care.

However, a good reply to a CMA is more than just a set of responses. It should be more like a personal letter to the learner. At least, it needs:

- an introductory bit
- a concluding bit.

The introductory bit can be the start of a letter. The computer is easily programmed to start a reply with 'Dear ...' filling in the learner's first name. Friendly remarks such as 'Thanks for sending in CMA 5' can be slotted in. General comments can be included, such as 'Most people find that Question 8 is the tricky one in this CMA.' If you're designing several consecutive CMAs, try to make their introductory bits different. The more 'human' the computer-generated letter appears to be, the better it serves your learners.

An introductory bit could look something like this:

Dear Jack,

Thanks for sending in CMA 5. Some of the questions in this Assignment were harder than they looked! Below, I've replied regarding the options you chose for each of the ten questions in turn. It would be useful to you to look again at the Assignment questions, to remind yourself of the choices you made.

The concluding bit can serve a variety of purposes. It can advise about the next assignment. It can give a general comment about the performance. For example, suppose there were ten questions in the CMA. There could be different concluding bits depending on score. A highly complimentary one could go to learners who got all questions right. A milder form of praise could go to learners who got 8 or 9 questions right. A strong message of encouragement may be needed by learners who got 2 or less right!

An example of a concluding paragraph is given below:

As you saw above, you got 7 out of the 10 questions right – that's good. All were right except the ones testing Section 5.8 of the module – it's worth you having another look at this Section I think. Otherwise, everything's splendid. The next CMA has ten questions on Unit 6. It's worth giving special attention to Section 6.3 – that's where most people have problems! Good luck – I look forward to CMA 6.

However, the heart of any CMA lies in the questions and responses. Chapter 3 should give you plenty of ideas regarding how best to make the computer feedback seem as human as possible.

Scores

We looked at this issue in some detail in Chapter 6; the same considerations still apply.

It's very easy indeed to instruct the computer to award a score. For example, the correct option to each question could score ten marks. A ten-question test would total 100, and the final score would conveniently look like a percentage.

Alternatively, some questions may be more important or difficult than others, and could be given scores to reflect this. Learners would need to know this as they made their choices.

But what about the incorrect options? It would be simple if they were all quite wrong, and scored zero marks each. But are they *equally* wrong? Or is there a next-best option, and might this be worth eight marks, or six marks – or *what?*

This is the problem with scoring multiple choice questions. Some options are better than others, and it's very hard to decide how much the less-than-perfect options should earn. If you want to score them, the best way of deciding how many marks to award to each incorrect option is to take the average of several people's opinions.

The final score can be built into either the introductory or concluding paragraphs of the computer-printed feedback.

For example:

Dear Sian,

  Thanks for sending in Assignment 3. Congratulations, you've scored 85 per cent. Please look below to remind yourself of all the things you did correctly, and to find one or two areas where you may like to refresh your memory.

or

Dear David,

  ... Now that you've explored the responses to your choices of options, it's time for your score – 55 per cent. That's just about a pass – but the important thing is you now know exactly which points you need to explore further.

It's still worth bearing in mind how the score can distract from the feedback, but that said, people do like to be given scores – especially good ones!

Other uses of CMAs

Gaining feedback *about* the learning materials

Think about the following sorts of question in CMA-form. (There wouldn't be a score to the questions below, of course.)

11. Which of the following did you personally find most helpful?
    A the SAQs and Responses
    B the Objectives
    C the text itself
    D the Review
12. Which Section do you think was the most successful in Module 3?
    A Section 1 on Causes of Corrosion
    B Section 2 on Prevention of Corrosion
    C Section 3 on Theory of Corrosion
    D Section 4 on Pourbaix Diagrams
13. In general, what is your opinion of the style of the materials?
    A easy to follow
    B fairly easy to follow
    C rather difficult to follow

       D very difficult to follow
14. How interesting did you find Module 3 in general?
       A very interesting
       B mostly interesting
       C sometimes interesting
       D rarely interesting
15. Approximately how long did it take you to study Module 4?
       A more than 10 hours
       B between 6 and 10 hours
       C between 3 and 6 hours
       D less than 3 hours

Such questions have the advantage that learners simply tick boxes or fill in letters on a simple form – quicker, easier and more anonymous than having to express opinions longhand. There are all sorts of similar questions which could be used to obtain feedback about chosen aspects of the learning materials. The computer could be programmed to build up files giving statistical analysis of the responses to each of the questions. This can make it much easier to assess objectively learners' views.

Although there may be no need for responses to such questions, it is possible to give useful comments as part of the computer-generated feedback. For example, let's take one of the questions above:

11. Which of the following did you personally find most helpful?
       A the SAQs and Responses
       B the Objectives
       C the text itself
       D the Review

The learner receives a response according to the option chosen. The purpose is simply to give the impression that his or her views are being taken into account, and that it was worthwhile choosing options. Of course, each learner sees only one of these responses:

11A We're glad you found the SAQs and Responses useful. They are opportunities for you to practise things, and to find out for yourself how you're getting on with your studies.
11B Good. You found the Objectives helpful. They are indeed intended to help you find out exactly what you need to be able to do to succeed in your studies.
11C We're glad you found the text useful. It may be worth trying to make more use of the SAQs and Responses, which are there to make sure you're getting enough practice at the things the text deals with.
11D We're glad you found the Review useful to you personally. Reviews can indeed be a quick way of reminding yourself about the main ideas in your

learning materials. Don't forget, however, to give yourself plenty of practice at *doing* things – that's what the SAQs and Responses are there for.

Gathering information about tutor support

The advantage of the CMA format is that learners are more willing to tick boxes or pick options than to express views about tutor support directly.

For example, the following questions could be asked:

16. How useful are you finding the feedback you receive on your TMAs from your tutor?
    A very useful
    B quite useful
    C not very useful
    D not at all useful

17. How do you feel about the time it takes to get TMAs back from your tutor?
    A feedback comes quickly
    B I'd like feedback more quickly
    C the delay is much too long
    D the delay doesn't really matter

18. How do you feel about your tutor?
    A my tutor is very helpful and encouraging
    B my tutor is quite helpful and encouraging
    C my tutor is not really helpful and encouraging
    D my tutor is quite unhelpful and discouraging!

19. How do you feel about the grades or scores your tutor gives?
    A very fair
    B fair enough
    C I don't feel they're fair
    D my tutor doesn't give grades or scores

While the purpose of such questions may be simply to gather information, it is still possible to reply to learners' choices with appropriate comments in CMA response style, so that learners are aware that their views have been noted.

Where several tutors are working in parallel, the sort of data collected through such questions can be useful in diagnosing tutors' strengths and weaknesses. Of course, it would be advisable to follow up any negative comments in more detail before drawing any firm conclusions – a learner may be prejudiced or unrealistic.

Helping learners

Of course, *everything* should be designed to help learners, but I'm thinking here of support with study skills development. For example, suppose the following question was included:

20. What are your present feelings about your forthcoming exam?
    A I'm scared stiff!
    B I'm rather apprehensive.
    C I'm becoming more confident.
    D I'm already confident.

Responses could give appropriate messages of sympathy or encouragement to learners selecting each of the options.

Conclusions

As we noted in Chapter 3, multiple choice questions have a somewhat tarnished reputation in educational circles, but they can serve many purposes as CMAs. As *feedback* questions they are very useful. Let's review briefly some of their advantages as the basis of CMAs.

1. The computer can respond very quickly to individual learners making different errors.
2. The computer doesn't get tired! The computer will patiently 'explain' the cause of a common mistake to as many learners as there are. Humans tend to get bored doing this – and take short cuts.
3. The computer doesn't get fed up of saying 'that's absolutely right' or 'don't worry, most of us have mixed this up at one time or another' or 'Question 5 was the hardest question in the set' and so on.
4. The computer can churn out a detailed set of feedback responses in a much shorter time than a human tutor. This means feedback gets to the learner much faster – before the questions have been forgotten! It's reckoned that the usefulness of feedback fades rapidly if it takes a long time to come. With SAQs the response can be immediate. With CMAs the response is still considerably faster than the average TMA feedback response.
5. Multiple choice questions can be used to gather information about how learners *feel* about many aspects of their studies. On some issues, learners may find it easier to pick options than to express their views openly. Responses to such questions can reassure learners that their views are being noted.

8. Selling the Benefits of Open Learning

Objectives

When you've thought about the ideas in this chapter, I hope you'll feel able to:

- accept that many people need persuading that open learning is a good thing
- sympathize with some of the reasons for hostility to open learning
- 'sell' open learning by translating its 'features' into 'benefits'.

I'm assuming that you've already got a good idea about what open learning is, and how it works, and that you yourself are fairly convinced that it is a good thing!

Let's regard open learning as our 'product', and use skills borrowed from the world of marketing to make the product as attractive and desirable as possible – not just to the consumers, but to everyone who may be involved.

We need to know what our 'product' is before we can start marketing it. Let's start by listing the main features of a good open learning system.

What are the main features of open learning?

- good use of learning objectives (see Chapter 2)
- self-assessment questions and responses (see Chapter 3)
- tutor-marked assignments (see Chapter 6) and maybe computer-marked assignments (see Chapter 7)
- learning materials that have been piloted and validated – not just any old set of notes
- materials which can be used in learners' own time, and in their own environment – home or workplace
- flexibility regarding pace
- user-friendly tone and style of materials (see Chapter 5)
- materials which may be retained by learners – who can re-learn from them any time the need arises.

The market

This list of features may mean a lot to people designing and implementing flexible learning programmes. But there are at least four groups in the 'market' – listed below – for whom a list of features will not convey enough.

- learners (students, trainees, etc)
- tutors (lecturers, trainers, instructors, etc)
- sponsors (employers, managers and so on who wish to have their personnel trained)
- training organizations (colleges, training centres, professional bodies and so on).

Each feature of open learning may have advantages for all of these groups, but those advantages may differ from group to group. The best way of interesting and attracting the person or group to whom you are 'selling' is to translate features into benefits. An effective way of doing this is to use the words 'which means that ...'. For example:

Open learning makes good use of learning objectives (*feature*) which means that you know what you're supposed to become able to do (*benefit*).

Let's look at 'objectives' in more detail.

FEATURE: *Good use of learning objectives*
Benefits for learners:

- – *which means that*
 you can see where the module is going to take you.
- – *which means that*
 you know what you're supposed to become able to do.
- – *which means that*
 you can see what you've mastered to date.
- – *which means that*
 you can identify which things you're going to need to do some additional work to master.

Benefits to tutors:

- – *which means that*
 you have learners who know where they're heading.
- – *which means that*
 you have learners who are aware of the things that they can already do.
- *which means that*
 you have learners who know the things where they need to do further work.

Feature	Benefits			
	for learners	for tutors	for sponsors	for training organizations
Good use of learning objectives (Chapter 2) *which means that . . .*	you can see where the module is going to take you.	you have learners who know where they're heading.	you can tell exactly how well a training programme fits the needs of your employees.	you can market your services on the expected outcomes of your programmes.
Self-assessment questions and responses *which means that . . .*	you can have as many go's as you like.	you have students who are doing a lot of the work and practice under their own steam.	you have employees taking more and more of the responsibility for learning on to their own shoulders.	you make better and more cost-effective use of your training staff – they're solving individual problems for more of the time, not just giving out information.

Figure 2 How different wording is needed to explain the same feature to different target groups

Benefits for Sponsors:

- ● – *which means that*
you can tell exactly how well a training programme fits the needs of your employees.
- ● – *which means that*
you can select the most suitable and effective training programmes.
- ● – *which means that*
you can get a measure of each employee's achievement in terms of his/her mastery of the programme's objectives.
- ● – *which means that*
you can tell what your people will be able to do after completing the open learning programme.

Benefits for training organizations:

- ● – *which means that*
you can market your services on the expected outcomes of your programmes.
- ● – *which means that*
you can test the effectiveness of the learning by measuring the achievement of the objectives.

FEATURE: *Self-assessment questions and responses*
Benefits to learners:

- ● – *which means that*
you can have as many go's as you like.
- ● – *which means that*
if you get the question right you'll feel good about it.
- ● – *which means that*
you can answer the questions at your own pace (and practise with them if you need to speed up ready for an exam or test).
- ● – *which means that*
if you make a mistake, no one sees you do it.
- ● – *which means that*
the responses will help you see where you go wrong.

Benefits to tutors:

- ● – *which means that*
you have students who are doing a lot of the work and practice under their own steam.
- ● – *which means that*
you spend less of your energy explaining to students where they're heading, and why.
- ● – *which means that*

you use less of your time in repetitive marking – your students measure their own progress for much of the time using SAQs and responses.

● – *which means that*

you spend less of your valuable time explaining the same mistakes over and over again – the SAQ responses do this for you.

● – *which means that*

you can spend more of your time dealing with individuals' particular problems.

Benefits to Sponsors:

● – *which means that*

you have your employees taking more and more of the responsibility for learning on to their own shoulders.

● – *which means that*

you allow your employees to become better learners – in future they'll learn things in a more self-sufficient way.

● – *which means that*

their training is more permanent – they keep their trainer – it's a module, not a transitory teaching-learning event.

● – *which means that*

you don't get so many discouraged employees because of 'failure' – most mistakes can be made in private and can be overcome well before any 'public' performance is required.

Benefits to training organizations:

● – *which means that*

you make better and more cost-effective use of your training staff – they're solving individuals' problems for more of the time, not just giving out information.

● – *which means that*

you have staff who waste less time on repetitive activities – including routine marking.

● – *which means that*

you produce students who are better at managing their own learning.

I could go on to do a similar exercise with all the remaining features. However, I expect you'll be able to do this rather better yourself – *you* know best the people you may need to convince about the benefits of open learning.

Why all this emphasis on 'selling the benefits'?

We need to sell the benefits because the move towards open learning often means considerable changes for those involved. The lecture room (or classroom) is often a place where the teacher feels safe – beyond the scrutiny of outsiders. Open learning may look a bit like 'going public'. Tutor-marked assignments, for instance, are permanent evidence of the work of the tutor who's doing a splendid job – and of the one who is not!

Developing open learning opportunities could involve slotting some self study elements into a 'conventional' programme (see p 26); or it could involve building some face-to-face work into something that had previously been run as a distance learning system.

Figure 3 shows you some of the possible reactions, objections and questions from the four 'market areas': learners, tutors, sponsors and training organizations.

Learners	Tutors	Sponsors	Training organizations
I'm suspicious of this new way of giving me greater responsibility for my own progress.	Am I losing the control I need?	It wasn't done like this in my day!	I'm wary of this notion of giving learners autonomy and freedom.

Figure 3 Some reactions to the prospect of being involved in open learning

Learners:

I'm suspicious of this new way of giving me greater responsibility for my own progress
Is it as good as a real course?
How will I know whether I'm doing alright?
Will it prepare me properly for the exam at the end?
Can I cope with working for much of the time on my own?
How do I get help when I need it?

Tutors:

Am I losing the control I need?
Does this mean I'm redundant?
But I *like* giving lectures!
How will I know that I'm doing my job properly if I can't be with my learners?

Sponsors:

It wasn't done like this in my day!
It can't be as good for them as sitting in classrooms?
Can they really learn without someone teaching them?
If there's no one standing over them, will they bother to learn?

Training organizations:

I'm wary of this notion of giving learners autonomy and freedom.
I'm worried that if we don't fill the seats in our classrooms people may infer that our courses are no good.

Conclusions

Once *you* are convinced about the usefulness of open learning, it may be your job to convince others – perhaps your senior colleagues. Perhaps you would like to go back to the list of features on p 98 and, bearing in mind your target group (or groups) turn each feature into as many benefits as you can. Armed with your knowledge of the 'target' and a good array of benefits, you are well equipped to overcome the scepticism and even hostility of others.

9. How to Tutor Open Learners

I'm assuming that you've already looked at Chapter 6, designing Tutor-marked Assignments. I'm also assuming that this has convinced you of:

- the importance of feedback, rather than just scores or grades
- the importance of objectivity in marking work
- the importance of making good use of model answers and assessment criteria.

In this chapter, I'd like us to explore the 'human' communication side of tutoring. This chapter is addressed directly to the open learning tutor. If you are *in charge* of tutors (rather than actually teaching) perhaps you can pass on the ideas I'm putting to you.

Objectives

By the end of this chapter, I trust that you'll be ready to be:

- an effective open learning tutor
- someone who makes a lot of positive difference to your learners' experiences of open learning.

What's involved in tutoring?

In this chapter I'm using the term 'tutoring' to cover a number of things. These include:

- assessment: marking assignment work and providing advice and guidance where mistakes have been made
- tutoring: providing tuition either face-to-face, or at a distance through written or telephone communication
- counselling: giving more general support and guidance, including helping open learners develop and maintain their motivation, and assisting them develop their learning skills.

Do open learners need tutoring?

If open learning materials were perfect, and if learners' learning skills were highly developed, there might be no need for tutoring. Even with imperfect learning materials, many learners soldier on and succeed without the help of a tutor. Many open learners have no choice – there just isn't a tutor anyway.

But most open learners would like some support. Even with the best of open learning materials, a good tutor can make all the difference to the learners' voyage. At the same time, it must be admitted that a poor tutor can do untold harm to learners' self-esteem and motivation. The essence of good tutoring lies in being responsive to learners' needs. A good starting point is to think about the learners themselves.

Who are open learners?

There may well be all sorts of different people studying your learning materials, but we must never forget that they're all individuals, each with their own hopes, fears, needs and ambitions. Having said that, there may be a few common characteristics:

1. *Keen to start.* Open learners tend to be high on motivation. They've usually made a definite decision – to start. Of course, *at any time* they can decide to *stop.* As a tutor, you've got to try and prevent them from stopping. Above all, you've got to make sure that anything you write to them or say to them doesn't turn out to be the last straw that breaks the camel's back!
2. *Good reasons for choosing.* Many open learners have chosen *not* to go for a more formal course of education or training. They won't want to be treated like schoolchildren but as experienced, responsible adults – they probably *are* experienced, responsible adults!
3. *Feeling vulnerable.* Many people who choose an open learning system have bad memories of conventional education. They may have experienced failure or have felt unable to make progress. Whatever subsequent experience they have gained, they may still be afraid when they return to studying.
4. *Needing help to work on their own.* For much of the time, they'll be working by themselves. They need to feel *involved* in their learning materials. You can do a lot to help this process, as discussed in Chapter 5, by using informal, friendly language.
5. *Have limited time to study.* The open learning programme isn't going to be the only thing in their lives! They may have full-time jobs. Many of your learners may have demanding families. They may have very limited time for studying. You can help them by breaking down their studies into *manageable chunks.* There are many more free ten-minutes spells in a busy person's week than there are free two-hours spells.
6. *Needing help in using textbooks.* Some of their learning may have to come from textbooks rather than from purpose-built open learning packages.

Many textbooks are relatively indigestible, and it can make all the difference if you can help them know exactly what they're supposed to be getting out of their textbook episodes. A few words of advice from you may turn what might have been an hour's passive reading into an hour's productive learning.

Making your own learner profiles

Still thinking of your learners as individuals, it's useful to build up profiles of the type of people who may be involved in your own open learning scene. You can do this by answering questions like these:

- Who is he/she?
- Why is he/she learning?
- Why has he/she chosen OPEN learning?
- What is his/her past experience?
- What are his/her main problems?
- How much time has he/she for studying?
- Has he/she any fears or anxieties?
- How does learning relate to the rest of his/her life?

Let's now go on to explore how learners *feel*. Of course, their feelings will change as their studies progress – and tutors will have to adjust accordingly. A good tutor will need a range of different skills to help learners through the different stages of their voyage.

Let's start at the beginning. This is the time when learners may decide that they're not equipped for the voyage. They may be quite wrong to decide this – and even when they're right, the good tutor can often find for them a voyage more suitable to their resources.

How does the open learner feel at the beginning?

Suppose it's the very first time that a person has tackled open learning. The learning package may look rather daunting – and at the same time stimulating. What sort of feelings has the learner got at the start of the programme? We can assume that they will be a mixture of the following:

- *Excited*. They may be expecting a lot. They may be very eager to get started – so eager in fact that there's the danger of skimming through any explanations regarding the best way of working through the package, preferring to dive in at the start of the subject material itself.
- *Apprehensive*. It may be the first time any learning has been attempted for some time (many years sometimes). Some learners feel a bit afraid of what they may have let themselves in for.

- *Curious*. Many will not have been *open* learners before. Such learners will need reassurance that it is indeed possible for them to learn under their own steam. They will need help in building confidence to organize their studies constructively.
- *Exposed and vulnerable*. The learning may carry with it some form of assessment; it may have been a long time since the learner had his or her work marked or graded. Some learners may have failed the last exam or assessment they took – perhaps many years ago. Many fear the 'judgements' to come!
- *Inadequate*. Many learners have doubts about their ability to succeed. The learning materials may look quite daunting – especially to those learners who skim ahead and see all sorts of things coming up that they have not heard of before. They may well be wondering 'Have I got to learn every word, diagram, chart and table in the material?' Of course they haven't got to learn the whole package – just achieve its objectives and answer questions up to a prescribed standard. But how can *they* tell this?

The above is obviously a generalization. It would be more useful to *ask* your learners how they feel – by phone or in writing. Giving learners the chance to open up to you can make a lot of difference in breaking down any barriers.

Learners' needs in mid-course

Learners often get 'mid-course blues'. Some of the novelty may have worn off, the subject matter is getting a bit harder, and the tutor may be getting a bit tougher as assessment targets become more important. They may now be feeling:

- *Fed-up*. The work's getting harder – and slower. The novelty's worn off. The path ahead seems like *work*, and *more work*.
- *Intimidated*. The material's getting harder. The assignments are getting tougher. The marks may be getting lower. How is everyone else getting on?
- *Pressurized*. The pace may be getting more 'forced'. Whatever happened to that 'freedom of pace' which was supposed to be the essence of open learning? But there's an exam coming up in 4 months ...
- *Alone*. Many learners may be feeling isolated – wondering if everyone else is having the same doubts, fears and even triumphs. It is very different from the class situation, where people so readily share their feelings and hopes. One of the biggest benefits of summer schools (as used in Britain, for example, in the Open University's foundation courses) is that learners quickly realize that they share many common problems, fears and hopes. Getting rid of that feeling of isolation can be a major boost to their morale.
- *Should I really have started this?* Life goes on. Other pressures – domestic, social, job – may all seem to be greater than ever. It's all too easy to give in and say 'I really haven't time to do all this learning as well.'

Again, of course, if learners have an open relationship with tutors, these feelings can be dealt with appropriately as and when they arise.

Learners' needs towards the end of the course

This is the time when they may well get frightened of forthcoming exams or assessments. They may need study skills advice relating to revision strategies and exam technique. It may be many years since they prepared for an exam. For some, their last experiences with exams may have been disastrous.

They may be unsure about what to do next. They may need your help in sorting out the options they have for further studies. Many open learners (despite any traumas!) become addicted to open learning – it becomes a valued part of their lives. They want to continue – and they want *you* to advise them what they can do next.

So, let's once again summarize their feelings.

- *Frightened.* Exams do this to people. Didn't it happen to you, years back?
- *Will I manage it?* They can become doubtful of their ability to overcome the next hurdles. 'What will people think of me if after all this time I don't succeed?'
- *Why should I bother?* The original aims of studying may not be so clear now. However, some good advice about what they can do after finishing the present course can provide useful motivation.
- *Time seems to be rushing by!* The exam date seems to get nearer so fast!

You don't have to be face-to-face with a learner to find out about these kinds of feelings. In fact the short note a learner encloses with an assignment is often the thing to look at most seriously.

Why concentrate on the negative feelings?

There will indeed be learners who suffer few if any of the negative feelings I've been listing. Your learners will include high-fliers who hardly seem to need your support at all. The high-fliers are a delight to work with – they may have bad moments but are more likely to be better able to fend for themselves.

Most of your energies and skills as a tutor are needed for those learners going through bad patches or problems, which is why I have gone into so much detail about how open learners feel.

Being able to help learners with difficulties has many rewards. One of these is that it keeps your *dropout rate* down. Your effectiveness as a tutor may be judged by some according to the dropout rate among your learners. Dropouts may not be your fault, but they might be *seen* to be your fault.

How can a good tutor help?

Set out in the following checklist are the sorts of help a tutor can give to learners as they work through an open learning programme.

- Make them feel at ease; be friendly.
- Build their confidence.
- Help them feel they're not alone.
- Convince them that their worries are common ones.
- Tell them you're there to help, not just to assess.
- Reassure them that most people make the mistakes they make.
- Open up channels of communication; first name, address, telephone numbers and so on.
- Take in what learners say to you in writing or on the phone. This takes conscious effort – it's easier to talk (or write) than to listen!
- Give study skills advice (but make sure it is suggestions rather than commands); help them start out on their studies in an organized, productive way.
- Remind them that even the hardest things can be mastered one step at a time.
- Bolster their egos when it comes to preparing for exams. Confidence may be as important as ability.
- Give practical advice regarding revision strategies and exam technique.
- Remind them that their present studies can lead them to choices and opportunities in the future.

Any good tutor will try to respond to all the problems and needs we have described. How you do this will depend on your circumstances. Of the three principal possibilities – in writing, by phone or face-to-face – only one or two may be available to you. Let's look at each one separately.

Written communication

This is the most common, and probably the most important means of communication between tutors and learners. There are two main kinds of written communication:

- written comments on marked work
- letters to learners, sent with marked work.

Comments written into learners' work
First, what colour should you use? Red? Green? Pencil? Think what you'd feel like if you wrote something, were proud of it, then got it back scrawled all over in red ink? Even if all the comments turned out to be congratulatory, the first sight of all that red would be demoralizing. If many of the comments were critical – need I say more?

Some learners are considerate enough to leave a wide margin, which serves as space for you to add comments and suggestions. If there's no such space available, you can write your comments on separate sheets, relating them to numbers or asterisks you slot into their work.

It's all too easy to put ticks and crosses. Obviously, crosses can be very demotivating. But even ticks can be improved upon. Here are a few words or phrases that warm open learners hearts!

'good point'	'that's the idea'
'I agree'	'spot-on!'
'quite so'	'that's the key one'
'indeed'	'I like this'
'you're right'	'a good example'
'I hadn't thought of this one'	

It makes all the difference to learners if they can see that you have read their work carefully. Such words or phrases speak louder than ticks in this respect.

Letters to learners

You'll probably need to write a brief letter with overall comment, every time you mark an assignment. It may well be entered into a space on a form, but its purposes remain the same as a conventional letter.

Why do learners need such letters? First of all, think of the feelings and emotions of the average open learner as he or she *reads* a letter from a tutor.

- Was it good enough?
- Have I made a fool of myself?
- Should I carry on?
- Did he/she really read my work?
- Is he/she trying to help me?

I can't tell you how to write the ideal letter! A letter is something from *you*. I can, however, remind you of some of the things that can go wrong.

Dangers to avoid in letters

There are words and phrases which a tutor might write, which would cause the learner's heart to sink. It's worth remembering that learners can be very sensitive, and using certain words with great caution.

One dangerous comment is: 'You've obviously put a lot of effort into this assignment.' Now this is alright if the learner *has*. But what if the learner *hasn't*? There goes the trust of the learner for the tutor!

Another comment to be avoided is: 'You have not quite grasped ...' or 'You don't seem to have understood ...' What does that do for the learner's self-esteem? Not a lot! None of us likes to have it implied that our understanding is at fault. We'd much rather read something like this:

Don't worry too much about ... Most people find this a difficult area. In fact, this topic causes more problems than most things. The textbook (or module) doesn't make it as clear as I'd like it to be. Please read the extra material I've enclosed, and do let me know if it helps or not.

Some danger words are more obvious, such as:

failed
error (slip, or mistake are milder somehow)
below the required standard (formal, threatening)
re-submit ('It would be worth you having another go' is more acceptable to learners)
unsatisfactory.

Of course, a balance needs to be struck between pandering to learners' feelings, and being honest regarding standards. In the very *first* letter to a particular learner, I'd advise caution. By the fifth letter you will probably know the learner well enough to know when to call a spade a spade.

I list below some characteristics of the best written communications to open learners. If you're involved in training/supervising open learning tutors, you may find it useful to apply this as a checklist to copies of some of their letters to learners.

Written feedback should be:

- friendly
- comforting regarding mistakes and problems
- helpful
- to-the-point
- informative
- not too critical
- not too hard
- informal
- constructive
- unambiguous
- easy-to-read and understand
  - short sentences
  - short words where possible
- motivating
- positive
- giving praise for things done well
- unpatronizing
- building rapport
- kindly setting standards for the future.

Written feedback should get to learners *as quickly as possible*. There's a lot of evidence that the value of the feedback goes down rapidly if there's much delay.

Learners may have moved on to other things, and the past assignment may be regarded as 'historical' if the feedback arrives weeks later! It sounds a tall order, but you should aim to mark and return work from open learners on the same day as you receive it.

Telephone communication

The telephone has several obvious advantages over the letter. First, you can have an immediate exchange of questions and answers. Second, it is easier to come across as a friendly human being on the phone. However, it is worth thinking about how to make telephone communication as effective as possible:

1. *Listen*. It's all too easy for you to say what you want to – at the expense of listening to find out exactly what the learner needs help with. Be sure to take time to listen.
2. *Be prepared*. It's useful to have your learners' records within reach. It can make all the difference if you can readily pull out a form or card with all the important information readily to hand. That's so much better than having to ask:

   > Who are you again please?
   > What was the last work you sent me?
   > What grade did I give you?
   > Is it you that has had a new arrival in the household?
   > Was it you that was having trouble with . . .?

   Your records should have little notes about all sorts of things beside assignments, dates, grades and names.
3. *Be available*. I don't mean 24 hours a day, seven days a week! What I'm getting at is letting your learners know 'good' times to ring you up. If you are caught at a bad time, 'Can I ring you back in half-an-hour?' is better than coming across disgruntled because you're in the middle of a meal.
4. *Make it worthwhile being phoned*. Naturally, any good tutor will answer the main question that a learner telephones about. It's better still, however, to give learners who ring you up that little bit extra – let them go away with the feeling that it was well worth ringing you up. This may lead to some extra phone calls for you, but it can help you to open up to your learners. After all, their success is your primary concern.
5. *Don't waffle*. Tempting as it is, if your learner asks you something you don't know, don't try to pretend you do. Your learner will respect you all the more for saying 'Sorry, I don't know – but I'll make it my business to find out, and get back to you.'
6. *Don't 'stick to your agenda'*. Here, I'm thinking mainly of occasions when you telephone a learner for a particular reason. It's all too easy for you to stick to that reason, when there may be other important things to deal with. It all goes back to the start of this list – being prepared to listen.

Face-to-face sessions

Some open learning schemes such as the Open University in Britain allow tutors and learners to meet. This has particular advantages in that learners can talk things over with each other, and overcome the isolation felt by many such learners.

The biggest danger with a face-to-face session is that the tutor comes prepared to *give* and not to *receive*. Conscientious tutors plan things to do at a face-to-face session – whether with individual learners or with a group. But over-preparation can result in tutors sticking too closely to their plans, and becoming impatient when anyone asks questions that take them off course.

If you've got a face-to-face tutorial session with a group of learners, get them *all* involved. There are all sorts of ways of doing this – all of which depend on breaking down formality, and allowing even the shyest in the group not to feel threatened or pressurized.

It helps a lot to sit your learners in a circle rather than in rows. That stops people at the back being excluded or cut off. If everyone in the group can see each other's facial expression, the group soon becomes more relaxed. If you're doing some 'input' now and then (for example, at a blackboard or screen), you may need a U-shape rather than a circle, but try to avoid rows.

In any face-to-face session, it's best to regard the *processes* as much more important than the *content*. I'm thinking of processes such as questioning, discussing, sharing ideas, solving problems and so on. All of these contribute to the learning process. If you were merely to provide a long lecture, there's no guarantee that much learning would occur. Think back to how boring many of the lectures you attended were!

All the things mentioned above regarding written and telephone communication apply also to face-to-face sessions. Please have another look through both the lists of suggestions given earlier, and think how you can build as many of them as possible into face-to-face sessions.

Conclusions

Good tutoring all comes back to thinking of each learner as a fellow human being. You should do everything you can to open up communication so that it isn't all one-way. Listening to learners, and reading their work (including between the lines) are perhaps more important skills than writing or speaking, if you're going to be seen by your learners as someone who gives positive support and help.

If your learners still send you Christmas cards years after their studies are over, you can regard yourself as a successful tutor.

10. Interactive Handouts – Open Learning Processes in the Lecture Room

This chapter is about extending the main principles and practices of open learning to the lecture situation. In particular, I'm thinking of lectures to fairly large groups of learners, such as are given in most colleges. Many college lecturers who've become involved in open learning (as writers or tutors, for example) report that they soon begin to approach lectures quite differently.

Objectives

By the time you've worked through this chapter, I hope you'll be better able to:

- describe the behaviour of learners in lecture sessions
- analyse learner behaviour in terms of activity or passivity.
- list some of the problems of lectures
- outline some advantages and disadvantages of issuing handouts in lectures
- describe how handouts can be made interactive
- design interactive handout material of your own.

The lecture situation

First, if you give lectures, I'd like you to answer a few questions. (If you don't give lectures, please think about how you'd answer these questions based on your past experiences in lecture rooms or classrooms.) Please be honest! Later in this chapter, I will be dealing with some typical answers to these questions, and you can compare your answers with these. Please don't read ahead yet!

1. What do your learners *actually do* for most of the time they spend in your lectures? (I *didn't* ask 'What would you *like* them to do?')
2. How much are your learners *learning* during your lectures? Go back through your answers to Question 1, and decide which of the verbs you used were 'active' and which were 'passive' in terms of learners *learning* during the lectures.
3. List three (or more) problems with the lecture situation. You can choose

to list problems your learners find with the lecture situation, or problems you find with it.
4. List some advantages of using handout material in lectures.
5. List any disadvantages of using handout material in lectures.

Lectures: content versus processes?

The traditional lecture tends to be dominated by the content. We feel comfortable if we have prepared the content. We feel relaxed if we know exactly what we are going to cover in a given lecture. We feel pleased with ourselves if we have mapped out the content for a forthcoming set of lectures. But what about the 'processes'?

There are two kinds of process to be considered: learning processes and teaching processes. Notice I put learning processes first. How much do our learners learn during our lectures? Do they learn everything we 'cover'? Think back. How much did *you* learn during lectures? Did most of your real learning in fact take place *after* the lectures? You may have used the notes you took out of the lecture room, but how often did you more or less start from scratch regarding the real learning?

Another way of looking at the traditional lecture is the 'transmit-receive' model. The lecturer 'transmits', the learners receive. But how good a transmitter is the average lecturer? Even the best transmitters are not always on peak form! More important, how good are learners at receiving? Does 'interference' often interrupt reception? Interference such as:

- 'resistance' – learners who are not feeling like receiving
- 'capacitance' – learners who are not able to receive well, because they're out of their depth, or just not on top form
- 'inductance' – learners who haven't been trained regarding how to get the most out of their lectures
- 'disconnection' – learners who for one reason or another are sitting there, but entirely 'switched-off'.

I often ask lecturers the question which I asked you to answer earlier: 'What do your learners actually *do* for most of the time they spend in your lectures?' I have had some surprising answers. Please compare your list with the one below which I have divided into 'active and 'passive' behaviour.

Passive	*Active*
Writing what you say	Asking questions
Writing from the blackboard	Answering questions
Copying from a screen	Calculating
Daydreaming	Discussing
Listening to you	Interpreting data
Fidgeting	Working out reasons

Watching you	Deciding what's important
Looking out of the window	Faultfinding
Talking among themselves	Making decisions
Doodling	Self-marking
Yawning	Thinking

Why are some of the chief activities passive?

Note that I've even got things like 'writing' as being passive. If learners are merely copying down something they see or hear, it can indeed be quite passive for them – ask them what they remember of what they've just written, if you doubt my point! I can well remember learning from lecture notes as exams loomed up – I couldn't remember a thing about the lectures, but there were my notes as proof I had actually been there!

Listening can also be passive. I admit it is possible to listen actively – a music enthusiast can listen actively, for example, paying attention to the speed, balance, interpretation and virtuosity of a performance. But in any music audience, a few members may be listening actively, and all the rest will be simply 'hearing' it. Of course, hearing can be very enjoyable. But we learn much less from things we merely hear, than from things we actively listen to. My point is that a lot of hearing goes on in most lectures, but not so much active listening. (And it's not easy to tell whether learners are hearing or listening – or doing neither!)

Some problems with lectures

Lecturers' problems

The lecturer is usually in control of the time, place, pace, style and content. But despite all this control, there can be problems:

1. It is not so easy to control the attention of the learners.
2. The focus tends to be on what the lecturer *wants to say*. This might be at the expense of what the learners *need to know*.

Learners' problems

1. Learners may fail to come to the lecture.
2. Learners can become bored or distracted by the topic or by the lecturer.
3. Learners may take notes, but the notes may be irrelevant, incomplete or illegible.
4. Learners may not follow up the lecture content – they may be too busy sitting in other lectures.
5. Learners may not be at their best during a particular lecture – got out of

bed the wrong side, have a hangover, not feeling 100 per cent, wrong time of the month and so on.

6. Learners may hesitate to ask questions when they can't understand something.
7. Learners may feel little sense of achievement, because of the passive role expected of them.

Advantages of using 'straight' handout material

From things I've said above, handout material may appear to solve a lot of problems. Thinking of the 'transmit-receive' model, handouts can mean that the learners have guaranteed reception. Or is it not as simple as this? Here are some advantages of using 'straight' handout material – the equivalent of an adequate set of lecture notes:

1. Each learner gets the same set of notes.
2. Learners don't have so much passive writing, copying and so on to do.
3. There should be more time for learners to think about the content of the lecture, rather than merely trying to write it all down.
4. Learners who are slow writers are less disadvantaged.
5. Learners who are weak in language skills are less disadvantaged – they have more chance to think about the content.

Disadvantages of 'straight' handout material

1. Learners may 'switch-off', secure in the knowledge that the handout material covers all they will need to master.
2. Learners may not come at all if they know they can get copies of handout material issued.
3. The handout material may be too extensive. It's only possible to write a few pages of notes in an hour; a handout can contain a dozen or more pages of printed material which may be too much to learn.
4. Sometimes handouts are no substitute for learners having done something themselves. This particularly applies to drawing, sketching, calculating, problem solving, decision making and so on.

Interactive materials and processes

Let's now look at how the problems of the lecture situation and the disadvantages of ordinary handout material can be tackled, using 'interactive' handout materials and 'interactive' processes during lectures.

What is an 'interactive handout'?

An interactive handout is more like a mini-open learning module than a set of lecture notes. It is a handout containing white space. Every now and then during a lecture each learner uses it to *do* something. A variety of lecture *activities* are structured around it. Even in a large group of learners, each one works independently at times during the lecture. I have used such handouts with groups of well over 100 learners, but most of the advantages also apply to much smaller groups as well.

Let's take for sake of argument a one-hour lecture slot. This is how I might use interactive handouts in such a lecture.

1. The handout, consisting of two to six sides of A4 size, is given to each learner at the start of the lecture. (Issuing them at the very start can help with punctuality problems. One can refuse to issue them to learners arriving ten minutes late! Or even more dramatic, such learners can be given pages 3 to 6, but NOT the first couple of pages, which may have already been 'done' in the first few minutes.)

2. The handout starts with a list of objectives. These are to give the learners a clear idea of 'where they should be' by the end of the lecture.

3. Every now and then, the handout is used to *elicit* information from members of the group. This can be arranged by posing questions towards the foot of a page, leaving two or three lines worth of blank space. The learners are given a minute or two to write down their answers. Then, the class is quizzed orally, and the correct answers sought from learners. The correct answers may already be printed in the handout, maybe at the top of the next page. If so, of course learners are asked *not* to read ahead (you can easily spot the odd one who turns a page before time!). This procedure is the lecture room equivalent of self-assessment questions and feedback responses.

4. Parts of the handout can be used for revision. Learners may be asked to answer one or two short questions about the earlier part of the lecture. The group is given a few minutes for each learner to have a go, then the answers are drawn from the group orally.

5. Now and then, the handout contains space for learners to *practise things*. There may be problems, and spaces for answers. A graph sheet may be included for the learners to plot data. These longer activities are best saved for the last third or so of the session. The tutor can then look over learners' shoulders, and help with particular problems.

6. Occasionally (but not too predictably), it's worth using part of the handout for revision of previous lectures. After the list of objectives, the first page may be given over to ten minutes' worth of questions and spaces. After the learners have attempted the questions, the correct answers can be drawn from the group. The learners can even be shown how to mark their own answers. Learners find it very useful to have this sort of accurate estimate of how well (or badly) they are doing. If a learner has done badly, he or she still has the comfort of not having been *seen* (except by closest neighbours perhaps) to have made mistakes. Besides, making mistakes and finding them out oneself is a good way of learning.

7. Once in a while, it's worth turning the final page or so of the handout into

a short test reviewing the content of the lecture just given, or the content of a few lectures. The test can be self-assessed by learners, or occasionally collected in and marked by their tutor.

Learners feel that handouts containing so much of their own efforts are very much more their own than any 'straight' handouts they may have been given. Learners get the same sort of psychological 'ownership' of their learning as occurs with good open learning materials. Even in the lecture situation, important bits of learning are being done under the learners' own control. I've seen learners go to considerable lengths to file and organize attractively their collections of interactive handouts, and even index them. I have yet to see an *interactive* handout being used as a paper aeroplane!

The art of quizzing the group

We've seen that interactive handouts are geared to allow learners to get involved with various things to do with learning processes. Let's now explore one aspect of the *teaching* process in which interactive handout material is useful.

Throughout this book I've concentrated on makings things as comfortable as possible for the learner. This bit may not be so comfortable, but it is useful for them – and you. Do it with a smile and a twinkle in your eye to keep the atmosphere friendly.

After giving learners the chance to complete a task and write down their answers to questions, the idea is to try to get *all* of them to the point of being ready to give an oral answer when asked. It's no use saying: 'Fred, what was your answer to Question 3?' – only Fred will think, and the rest will have a chance to switch off.

Think about the effect of altering the process as follows. Ask everybody: 'What is the answer to Question 3?' Pause and look around. Then pounce! 'Fred?'

Even better, don't actually look at your 'victim' as you call his or her name.

But what if you don't know their names? Even with a large group, it is possible to get each member to have answers ready. If a number is pencilled onto the top corner of each handout, you can pick random numbers, and ask the owner of that handout for an answer. If the owner tries to remain anonymous, a neighbour can usually be relied on to give him or her away! If the same number comes up again from time to time, even someone who has already answered a question isn't 'safe' and must remain alert.

Interactive handouts: solving lecture problems

Let's recall each of the lecture and 'straight' handout problems and see the solution offered by interactive handouts:

1. *It is very easy for learners to remain passive or switched-off for much of the time.*

   It is not at all easy if they are frequently being asked to respond, both in writing and orally. They are also making decisions for much of the time, for example: 'What is the important point I'm supposed to write in this blank space?'

2. *It is easy for the lecturer to believe that he or she is being understood, when the truth may be very different. Learners become good at looking as though they are understanding everything, especially when they are not!*

   The lecturer can measure the progress of learners from their oral responses to questions, and can look at what learners have written in their handouts in answer to questions, and so on. The lecturer can then go over things that are causing problems, right at the time when the 'owners' of the problems are receptive to help.

3. *In an ordinary lecture the lecturer may not notice real difficulties being experienced by learners.*

   If few pens are in motion when learners are asked to jot something down in their handouts (for example, the answers to questions), the lecturer immediately knows learners are having difficulty. The nature of any difficulties is revealed when individual learners are asked to say what they have written in their handouts.

4. *If ordinary handout material is issued, learners often switch off secure in the knowledge that they have already got a set of notes. This happens even when the handout is not adequate as a set of notes.*

   The interactive handout when issued is far from a complete set of notes. It *becomes* a complete set of notes by the end of the lecture. But the most important ingredient of that set of notes is the input from the individual learner. Learners quickly realize that the printed handout is not much good as it stands. They see that their task during the lecture is to turn it into something that will be useful to them during their future learning.

5. *Learners in large groups who know that ordinary handouts are regularly issued are often tempted to miss lectures, because they won't be missed and they can get copies of colleagues' handouts later.*

   With interactive handouts, the important part of each lecture is what the learners DO. A blank, empty handout is not much good, and does not help a learner catch up on a missed lecture.

6. *When learners come to revise material given in lectures, they often have to start their learning from scratch, remembering little of the actual lecture.*

   My own feedback from learners who worked through interactive handouts in lectures, shows that they feel that they did a lot of learning *during* the lectures. They feel that they are far from starting from scratch when they come to revise. They often admit that they are more tired after an interactive lecture, but a lot less bored!

7. *It is difficult for even the best lecturer to keep all learners in a group 'abreast' through a lecture. Some will lag behind the lecturer, others will be ahead. Concentration-spans are much shorter than lecturers would like them to be!*

   With interactive handouts, each individual activity takes a relatively short time. There is less chance for concentration to wane. A change can be as good as a rest!

'Devil's advocate'

The interactive kind of lecture represents a big departure from the traditional public performance lecture. As few people accept changes easily, many objections have been raised to the interactive handout. I've listed a few of them here, together with my counter-argument:

1. *It takes too long to give this much thought to designing handouts.*
   Yes, It takes time at first, but designing and producing handouts are essentially skills, and it becomes faster and easier with practice. Then, it begins to *save* time: it is far easier to make adjustments or additions to a couple of pages of an interactive handout, than it is to rewrite parts of a handout which is continual text. The blank spaces give considerable flexibility.
2. *Learners wouldn't like them.*
   Learners do in fact like them, because they soon find how much more they are learning *during* lectures - and how much less they need to do after lectures to consolidate the material. They also comment that 'the time flies in lectures when we're doing something every few minutes'.
3. *It costs too much - all that extra paper, for example!*
   Yes, indeed, a six-page interactive handout costs more to produce than a two-page straight handout (or no handout at all). But if interactive handouts prove to be an effective means of promoting learning (*during* lectures as well as later) surely that in itself justifies the extra cost. Besides, if interactive handout materials are produced in bulk well ahead of each lecture, it may be cheaper than notes hastily photocopied a few minutes before the lecture starts!
4. *It's closing-up learning.*
   People who say this are usually implying that interactive handout material sets the agenda for each lecture too rigidly, and that chances are lost to explore topical subjects or issues arising spontaneously during lectures. But the lecturer still has control. 'Let's leave the handout for ten minutes' may even be a welcome suggestion.

From lecture notes to interactive handouts

It's not too difficult for a lecturer to translate his or her own lecture notes into an interactive handout. This can also be a first stage of transforming lecture notes into open learning materials. The main processes involved are:

- deleting quite a bit of the detail - detail the learners don't need to *remember*, merely talk about and *think about* during the lecture
- adding *blank spaces* for learners to do important things with. This is very easy!
- writing short, simple *brief* so learners know what exactly they should with each blank space. It's better to have such briefings printed in the handout than to rely on giving them orally during lectures - there's something about

a written brief which seems to make it more likely that everyone will be trying to tackle the same task.

- designing revision tasks and so on, to form parts of the learning process during the lecture
- providing a clear set of objectives for each lecture at the start of each handout. (It's often easier to pin down the exact objectives *after* you've mapped out what learners will be doing during the session). The objectives can be reiterated at the end of the handout for learners to check on what they have learned.

Conclusions

If you can do all the things set out as objectives for this chapter, I'm sure your learners will be getting a lot from your lectures. You too may feel that your time in lecture rooms is being well spent. What's more, you'll have realized that lectures and open learning are not completely different things; they are both part of the same business – the facilitation of learning.

11. Adult Entry to Science and Technology

This chapter is intended for authors writing open learning materials in science and technology subject areas. It's also intended for people who may be supporting open learners in these disciplines.

There has always been a sort of culture-gap between two main categories of subject matter:

- arts: languages, history, social studies, legal studies, business studies, management and so on.
- science: technology, engineering, mathematics, computing, and so on.

Increasingly, people who have had a training in one category find themselves, for one reason or another, plunged into the other category. This often happens to them in mid-career, when they need the 'new' discipline to advance their career.

It seems surprisingly easy for people who have had a science/technology/ engineering training to take to arts subjects such as business or management studies. The reverse transition – from arts to science – seems to be more painful. Many reasons can be advanced to explain this state of affairs. However, in this chapter I'd like simply to examine some of the problems, then propose some solutions.

Objectives

When you've explored this chapter, you should be able to:

- appreciate the problems which many adults experience when studying (for the first time) science or technology subjects
- respond to their problems, enabling them to have a more comfortable introduction to science or technology.

Problems adults experience when beginning to learn science and technology subjects

Culture Shock

Adults being confronted with science for the first time since schooldays experience a culture shock. They feel 'illiterate' in 'alien languages' of physics, chemistry and mathematical equations. Adults find it especially difficult to *write* in the new language or terminology. It's one thing to look at and understand equations and formulae, it's much harder to write them.

Whereas in arts subjects intuition and life experience can help a lot, in science subjects new students may not find these natural resources useful. They may indeed be resistant to scientific facts and concepts.

Children are more able to take on scientific ideas: they accept them as part of a game, a game led by teachers. Children will memorize things, apply them, get 8 out of 10 and be quite content to do so. Adults will not be content if they don't *understand* everything. They want to understand things right away. Often this isn't possible. And they get worried.

'I feel insecure'

Adult learners going into science or technology for the first time feel they are taking a risk. They are sensitive about their ignorance and are afraid of losing their self-respect.

'When I don't understand something, can I say so?'

It takes a lot of courage for an adult to say 'I don't understand'. Such a statement should never be treated lightly by tutor or lecturer. An adult making this statement is never joking! It is a well considered call for help. When help is offered, it must be done very carefully. 'Remedial' tuition will be perceived by adult newcomers to science as a clinic for stupid people! A child who doesn't yet know something rarely feels stupid. An adult tends to!

'An awful lot depends on this course.'

Adults starting to study science usually have strong professional reasons. This makes them highly motivated and demanding; it also gives them the feeling that their whole being is at stake. They object strongly if they feel their time is being wasted – they are usually busy people. Very few adults who start science for the first time do so simply for the sake of learning.

'Will there be any 'live' tutorials?'

It is a sad fact that science tutorials/classes, unlike arts ones, tend to sit learners in rows, with little interaction between them, and learners feel isolated. This difference between science and arts training is one reason why many adults prefer to enter science and technology via open learning rather than conventional systems.

'When will I get to the bit that I want?'

Science programmes contain many elements and tutors need to help learners see why each element is there and how it is relevant. The sequential nature of subject matter in science and technology can cause difficulties if learners don't realize that they must understand even material they may find uninteresting before they will be able to move on to a subsequent stage of learning.

'Do I really need these prerequisites?'

Most good open learning packages spell out any prerequisite knowledge or skills. Learners are often unwilling to accept these, but with science and technology, they are often essential and in no way optional.

'Do I really need the support of a tutor?'

One-to-one tuition is needed more by adults starting in science, than by most other sorts of learner.

Of course, it's not all problems! Adults who really 'get into' science find that their whole life experience is enriched with a greater 'Riding a bike' understanding of everything around them. It's quite important for people supporting adult learners in science and technology to be able to show how the features of the learning programme can benefit them. (We explored this sort of idea in Chapter 8.)

Some answers and remedies

I'll briefly discuss half a dozen areas where we can help adults starting on science/technology programmes. These are:

- study skills assistance
- open learning materials
- entry points for adult learners
- tutor-development
- assessment criteria
- feedback from learners.

Study skills assistance

Adults starting out on science and technology studies often need – and want – help with the following:

- managing their time efficiently so that study can fit in

- preparing for assessment of all sorts
- mapping out the particular problems and challenges they will meet with their science and technology subjects
- developing methods for tackling these problems
- developing self-confidence
- improving self-sufficiency as learners.

Of course, most learners benefit from this sort of help – whatever their subjects or ages. However, I feel that study-skills assistance is particularly valuable to adults learning science and technology for the first time.

Open learning materials

Good quality open learning materials can help sort out the mess regarding pre-requisites, starting levels, confidence and so on.

A good module will include plenty of self-assessment exercises and responses; the adult learner can fail with the comfort of privacy until he or she succeeds.

Entry points for adult learners

Adults don't like to be assessed before they start out on their science studies. They don't want to be tested on what they don't yet know. However, they are perfectly capable of testing themselves if we give them the tools. We could help them prepare for an entry point as follows, for example.

Have a go at these pre-tests with the comfort of privacy. If you get more than 70 per cent when you mark your answers, you don't need to do component x of the course – and so on. If you get less than 70 per cent, you can join the group taking component x (or you can use the self-study module for that topic). Don't worry if you don't get all the answers right. In the brown envelope you'll find full explanations of the questions and answers concerned – but don't look at these before you have a go yourself, of course.

Tutor-development

Most science tutors dealing with adults entering the subject for the first time could improve their efforts in the following areas:

- Avoiding assumptions
    between tutor and learners
    between learners themselves
    about the subject matter
    about aims and objectives
    about assessment criteria
- aiding constructive group dynamics
- achieving effective communication
- appreciating the culture shock

- building and maintaining the self-esteem and confidence of adult learners.

With improvement in these areas, learning should take place effectively and enjoyably.

Assessment criteria

Tutors in science, technology and maths are usually well-versed in devising examinations, and accompanying marking schedules. The criteria for gaining or losing marks are of immense interest to adult learners (and to any students in fact). Yet all too often, assessment criteria are kept private, confidential, even 'top secret'!

If assessment criteria are kept 'on the table' throughout tuition, adult learners gain a lot from the criteria themselves. They learn what it takes to be successful. They learn the rules of the game. They learn how the system works. They develop their confidence in the system.

If learners themselves are given the chance to apply realistic assessment criteria to their own efforts, they have the comfort of making mistakes without being seen by others. Then when real assessment comes along, they have learned from their mistakes, and can suceed. Moreover, they *expect* to be able to succeed – the exam is no longer the great unknown.

Feedback from learners

It is – not before time – becoming more usual to seek feedback from 'the customers' of education and training – the learners. Questionnaires can provide a lot of feedback – quickly – and in a non-threatening way as far as learners are concerned. Adult learners are well able to express their reactions through questionnaire responses and comments.

If feedback is sought early, often, and regularly, tutors have every chance to adjust and adapt their approaches to meet the needs of their adult learners. For too long, an hour's learning or tuition has meant an hour's worth of content. If a mere five minutes of every hour were structured to provide learner feedback (oral, written, whatever), programmes could be improved very thoroughly and effectively.

Conclusions

What we've said in this chapter applies to adult entry into science and technology courses of all kinds. In every science and technology course there will probably be at least some 'live tuition' in workshops, laboratories and classrooms. I think the problems of adult learners need to be appreciated by those involved in such tuition.

Many of the main principles of open learning are particularly helpful to adults returning to study science and technology.

12. Editing Open Learning Materials

This chapter is designed to help people involved in editing open learning material. It is also intended to be of use to authors of such material, in reminding them of the principal criteria which will be applied to their draft material.

Objectives

When you've explored this chapter, you should be able to:

- recognize four kinds of editing
- 'educationally-edit' open learning materials.

Educational editing

In this chapter I'm addressing 'educational' editing. There are other kinds of editing, all of which are important, but which do not concern us here. Let me briefly describe them.

Copy editing. This simply involves things like grammar, spelling, punctuation and so on. It's useful to get another pair of eyes to look at draft material, as the author tends to be the last person to spot this kind of error. The author reads what he or she *meant* to say! A good typist is a better copy editor than most authors.

Technical editing. This involves making sure that the material is factually correct. Technical editing is normally undertaken by people who are experts in the topics covered by the material. Technical editing can be 'bought in' fairly easily and cheaply. Technical editors do not normally undertake 'educational' editing as well, unless they have had training in design of open learning materials.

Housestyle editing. Most open learning projects conform to an agreed style. This involves agreed use of white space, page layout, indenting, headings, boxes, colour, flags (eg for self-assessment questions, activities and so on). Housestyle editing is concerned with appearance and does not usually involve major changes to the words of the material.

The educational editor may well contribute towards all these tasks but is concerned principally with making sure that the material *works* in open learning mode. It may involve major changes in 'raw' material (unless authors have already had substantial training in the design of such material).

Educational editing will often involve changes or improvements regarding things like:

- objectives
- self-assessment questions and activities
- responses to SAQs and activities
- summaries and reviews
- visual elements (diagrams, graphs, pictures and so on).

Educational editing does not involve changes to the technical or subject content, but may well involve changes to the way it is structured and presented.

The role of the educational editor is not just to cross things out, or indicate things that are missing. It is to diagnose weaknesses, remove them and replace them with something better.

How *not* to do an educational edit

It's very tempting to read someone else's work and say to yourself: 'Oh dear, that's not how I would explain this myself.' But it doesn't have to be anything like how you would do it yourself.

The question that really matters is: 'Will it work, just as it stands?' If it works, there's no need to make serious changes, even if you would prefer to see it done a different way. No two people write in the same style; – we may feel our own is superior, but it probably isn't.

Remember that every time an editor makes serious changes to an author's work, the author becomes discouraged – and may give up.

It's useful to remind yourself that the open learning material is not aimed at you. It's probably aimed at people with a great deal less experience/knowledge than you. So things that you find simple may be difficult for the average learner. There will be times when you feel patronized, but the average learner won't.

It's important, therefore, that serious changes are made only when the material would not function well as open learning material in its existing form.

Educational editing of open learning materials necessarily focuses on the main features of such materials: objectives, self-assessment questions and responses, activities and summaries.

At the same time, there is the issue of tone and style. The tone should be such that people working entirely on their own are welcomed into the material, and kept as motivated and active as possible. That means it should be reasonably friendly and informal (without being patronizing).

It is also essential that nothing is ambiguous. People working on their own are in greater danger than others of misunderstanding what was intended and trying to proceed along the wrong path. Keeping sentences short is one way of avoiding ambiguity.

In the checklist below, I address each of the main features of good open learning material, and suggest what educational editors should try to do when they find the material lacking.

Checklist for educational editing

1. *Objectives*

- Are they stated clearly and unambiguously? If not, rephrase them.
- Are they presented in a friendly way rather than a formal way? If not, making sure they contain the word 'you' may be a good start towards improving them.
- Do they contain jargon which may not be known to the learner before starting the material? If so, can it be explained or omitted?

2. *Self-assessment questions and activities*

- Are there plenty of them? If not, can you add some additional ones here and there – even short ones?
- Are the tasks set by the questions clear and unconfusing? If not can you adjust the wording to help learners know what they're supposed to do?
- Are the questions and tasks inviting? Is it clear to learners that it's valuable for them to have a go rather than skip? If not, can you 'warm-up' the question with a few words of encouragement?
- Collectively, do the SAQs and activities test the learners' achievement of the objectives? It's alright to have some SAQs and activities which go beyond the objectives, as long as the learner is told about this. The danger is that some objectives are *not* covered by SAQs and activities. You may need to try to bridge any such gaps you identify by composing SAQs and responses.

3. *Responses to SAQs*

- Is it really a *response* to what the learner has done (ie not just an answer to the question)? This is where most editing is usually needed; you may often find yourself translating an answer into a real response. After all, the learner at this point wants to know: 'Am I right? If not, what went wrong and what do I do about it?'
- Does the response include encouragement or praise (without patronizing) for the learner who got it right? If not, it's easy enough to add a few appropriate words.
- Does the response include something that will help learners who got

it wrong *not* to feel like complete idiots? A few words such as 'This was a tricky question' or 'Most people find this hard at first' and so on, can make all the difference to learners who got it wrong.

4. *Summaries or reviews*

- In good 'live' teaching, we usually make principal points at least twice. We might say: 'Another way of looking at this is ...' or 'Let me remind you that the main point you need to remember is ...' Open learners need similar focusing.
- Are there *frequent* summaries or reviews, reminding learners of the main issues they should now know? If not, it could be useful for you to add in a few lines here and there under a sub-heading 'Review' or 'Summary'.
- Is it possible to turn the summaries into an *activity* for learners? For example:

  Now that we've finished Section 3, check that you feel confident regarding:

  Defining ...
  Describing ...
  Explaining ...
  Calculating ...
  Measuring ...

5. *The text itself*
   In my view, the text is less important than the things already addressed in this checklist. However, it still requires your close attention.

- Is it readable and unambiguous? Do you need to

  simplify
  replace any long words with shorter ones
  reduce the length of long sentences?

- Is it relevant, keeping to the objectives as stated? If text is rambling, you may be able to delete sections without losing logic or coherence.
- Is it 'involving' where possible? Is there plenty of use of 'you' for the learner, 'I' for the author, and 'we' for the learner and author together? It should not read like a textbook or manual.

6. *Diagrams, pictures, charts, tables, graphs and so on*
   These are firmly on the agenda for educational editors! Visuals are often the places where dangerous errors creep in.

- Is it as self-explanatory as possible? If not, a few labels, or additional words in a caption can make all the difference.
- Does the learner know what to do with it, ie to learn it, note it in passing, do nothing at all, pick out the trend and so on? If not, it only takes a few words to give the learner helpful advice.
- 'A sketch can be more useful than 1000 words.' Is the material sufficiently illustrated? If not, you may be able to sketch some additional illustrations (or go back to the author for some).

7. *General points to look for*

- Is the introduction warm and welcoming? It only takes a few friendly words to make an introduction much more attractive.
- If there are any prerequisites, are they spelled out clearly before the start? 'This module assumes that you've already done ... which was contained in Module 2' is the sort of wording that can help.
- Is sensible advice given about *how* to use the material? For example, a few words about the benefits of having a go at each of the tasks may need to be added.
- Is the material broken down into manageable chunks coinciding with learners' concentration spans? You may need to break down any long sections of material.
- Are there any sudden jumps in level? These can put learners right off, unless they're given advance warning. So, if the jump is really necessary, precede it by, for example: 'Now the next bit is much more difficult. Take your time with this. Look at the next paragraph at least three times before trying the SAQ which follows it!' If learners are warned that something is tough, they pull out all the stops to try and master it.
- Does the material ensure that the average learner will be able to achieve the objectives? This is hard for an editor to tell – the real test comes with the pilot run of the material.
- Will the average learner *enjoy* using the material? (If learners enjoy using the material, they're going to spend more time with it, more willingly. The success of their learning is of course directly linked to the time they spend at it.)

Conclusions

Editing is not just a matter of pointing out things you don't like. To do a useful editing job on open learning materials, you need to be able to replace such things by something better.

Sometimes, you need to be well versed in the subject matter, perhaps to have a lot of experience of teaching it, to do a good editing job. For example, in subjects like mathematics, to respond to an SAQ, you need to be well aware of the most probable errors or difficulties.

In many other subjects, however, it's possible to do a useful editing job (in collaboration with the author, of course) without being a subject expert. In fact, it can be useful to be learning the subject as you edit – you may be able to spot problems that the author hadn't thought of.

13. Choosing and Using Open Learning

This chapter is a list of 64 key questions to help you to judge the quality and suitability of any open learning materials you already have or may want to use. The questions can also be used to help decide where it is worth the time and effort to adapt existing materials to meet the needs of known groups of learners.

Alternatively, reading through the 64 questions could be a quick way of reminding yourself of the main features of good open learning materials and systems.

Checklist areas

The questions are split into specific areas as shown below (some areas may be directly relevant to your particular circumstances, others not):

- interaction (SAQs, activities, responses and so on)
- objectives
- text: tone and style
- diagrams, etc (including tables, pictures, charts, graphs, cartoons and so on)
- study skills help
- use of media
- assessment (assignments, tutor-support and so on)
- miscellaneous key issues

The checklist questions are designed to have 'yes' or 'no' answers. Which answer is best will depend on the needs of your learners, and the level of the learning programme. If the answer to a question is 'no' when you'd want it to be 'yes', it may be quite easy to add things to the materials or change things. If it isn't easy, it may be necessary to look more critically at whether the materials will meet the needs of your learners.

Interaction

- Will learners be kept sufficiently active as they work through the material?

- Are there spaces for learners to write things into the material?
- Are there sufficient SAQs?
- Are there other activities?
- Are there real responses to SAQs and activities, not just mere answers?
- Is each main learning objective well covered by SAQs and responses?
- Are SAQs and activities interesting and inviting?
- Are responses out of sight of the SAQs?
- Do the responses help the learner who made a mistake find out exactly what the mistake was?
- Do the responses give praise (in an appropriate, non-patronizing way) to learners who get SAQs right?
- Will you need to devise additional SAQs and responses to improve the material?
- Will learners have a realistic idea of how well (or otherwise) their learning is going?

Objectives

- Are they clearly stated?
- Is it clear what learners should already be able to do before starting? (ie Is prerequisite knowledge/experience clearly explained?)
- Are they unambiguous?
- Will they help learners find out exactly what they are going to try to achieve?
- Will they be directly useful to learners?
- Do they give a good idea of what training the package should accomplish?
- Are they directly relevant to the needs of your learners?
- Is it possible to test learners' achievement of the objectives?
- Do SAQs, activities and responses give learners the chance to test their own achievement of the objectives?

Text: tone and style

- Is the tone and style friendly and informal?
- Is the introduction stimulating and welcoming?
- Does the material relate directly to the needs of your learners?
- Might it be necessary to select parts of the material for your learners?
- Does the text relate directly to the stated objectives, without going off at tangents too often?
- Is there plenty of 'active' language like 'you', 'I', 'we' and so on?
- Is the text easily readable (both in terms of clarity on the page, and level of language used)?
- Is the material broken down into manageable chunks (ie no extended areas of solid text)?

- Are main ideas suitably reviewed at the end of each part of the material?
- Are reviews turned (where possible) into something active that learners can do?
- Is the material well 'signposted'? (ie Do learners know where they're heading, where they are now, and where they've come from?)

Diagrams etc

- Are there sufficient illustrations to make the material visually interesting?
- Are all diagrams etc self-explanatory within reason?
- Are captions complete and informative?
- Are learners told what the expectation is of them regarding each illustration (to become able to reproduce the illustration, or merely to recognize it, for example)?
- Are diagrams properly labelled?
- Are illustrations sufficiently large (ie not thumbnail sketches)?
- Has care been taken to ensure that diagrams (charts, graphs, tables etc) are visible when reading the text that is directly connected with them (ie avoiding the learner having to turn pages backwards or forwards too often)?

Study skills help

- Is there clear advice on how best to use the materials?
- Is this given as a separate document or as the introduction to the first module?
- Will you need to prepare your own guidance material?
- Does the material help learners with suggestions regarding how best to approach important topics as they come up?
- Might it be necessary for you to provide a suitable induction programme to guide learners regarding use of the material?
- Will it be necessary for you to provide tutor support (or counselling, 'mentors' etc) to help learners who have problems when using the material?

Use of media

Open learning materials may use several media, or may be entirely print-based. The questions below are intended to help you ensure that any non-text media in your packages are being used appropriately. 'It' can refer to video, audio tape, practical kit, computer etc.

- Is the learner using 'it' actively (ie not just watching a video then quickly forgetting it)?

- Does 'it' do something in a better way than less expensive media (eg print)?
- Does the learner know what to get out of 'it'?
- Does the learner know why 'it' is present with the materials?
- Will 'it' limit when and where the learner can use the materials? (For instance, if material depends strongly on video tape, the learner will only be able to learn when and where there is access to suitable playback equipment.)
- Is 'it' enjoyable to use/watch/listen to?
- How useful is 'it' to the learners in achieving the objectives of the material?
- Would it be necessary for each learner to possess 'it', or could a single one serve a number of learners?

Assessment

Some open learning materials can be bought with tutor support included, others include tutor support as an option. Alternatively, you may wish to organize your own tutor support, or the materials may need no support. This list of questions is to remind you of some of the issues and choices involved.

- Is the material designed for tutor support?
- Are assignments built into the material at appropriate places?
- Might you need to design assignments for your learners to do at appropriate points?
- Will you provide tutor support?
- Can you have/will you use tutor support from elsewhere?
- Does the material prepare learners for some recognized qualification (ie is it tied to a particular syllabus and standard)?

Miscellaneous key issues

Suppose you've identified some open learning materials, and appraised their qualities using the above lists of questions. These are a few more key questions you may want to consider.

- Is it good value for money?
- Is it up-to-date and authoritative?
- Can I get access to some people who have used the material already, and seek their comments?
- Can I get access to people who can tell me how effectively the materials achieved their purpose (eg supervisors of past learners)?
- Have I checked that I have seen all the materials (from different providers) which are likely to be relevant, before choosing?

Conclusions

If you applied this checklist to a piece of open learning material and got the answer you wanted to every question, you would, I suppose, have found an example of open learning at its very best. However, as we've seen in other chapters of this book, there is often help available to open learners – from tutors, for example. So it's perfectly possible for some material to be used successfully, even if it falls short of several of the criteria listed.

What you are looking for, when it comes down to it, is fitness for purpose (at reasonable cost).

14. Open Learning: A Catalyst for Staff Development

I'd like to use this chapter to remind you of some of the key ideas I've been proposing throughout this book, and to link them to staff development.

I look at some of the effects that getting involved in open learning can have on college lecturers, or trainers in commerce and industry. I outline ten ways in which getting involved in open or distance learning can cause staff development to take place. The staff development that occurs has favourable implications for traditional sorts of study too. It also has the considerable advantage of occurring as a by-product of other activity, rather than as the result of a direct attack on inadequate teaching performance.

It should not, however, be assumed that all teaching/training staff who get involved in open learning suddenly become much better: some don't; some never will!

Objectives

You may find ideas in this chapter which will help you to:

- identify your personal development needs as a teacher/trainer
- use involvement in open learning to develop staff under your control.

Close encounters with open learning

There are several ways that teaching staff can get involved with open learning, including:

- directly, as open learners
- by designing open learning materials
- by using open learning materials with their own learners
- by tutoring open learners
- by setting up an open learning resource centre
- by managing open learners.

What features do we find in *good* open learning materials and systems? Let me remind you of some which contrast markedly with more traditional things such as textbooks, manuals or lectures.

- user-friendly style
- 'personal' involvement of learners
- purposes clearly identified and explained
- activity-based systems
- emphasis on processes rather than content
- feedback on success or problems
- learning styles firmly on the agenda.

As we saw in Chapters 6, 9, 10 and 11, there's more to good open learning than well designed materials. Open learning can be made much better with good support of one kind or another. Even quite poor open learning materials can be made to work well, with skilled and responsive tutor back-up. Tutors can supply whatever is lacking in the materials. To our list of features can be added three features of good open learning tutoring/counselling:

- ability to communicate with learners at a distance in letters and comments on assignments, and on the telephone
- ability to deal with *individuals'* problems and needs
- ability to compensate open learners for the lack of interaction with other learners.

Staff development implications

The ten principal features of open learning materials and systems listed above are not given in any particular order of priority, and they overlap with each other to some extent. My point is that each of these features can lead to the development of skills that can usefully be transferred to the classroom or lecture room. These skills can lead to more effective learning in conventional teaching/ learning contexts.

Many teaching staff who have become intimately involved in open learning admit that they now do things differently in their 'normal' teaching. That's why I think it's worth exploring each of our ten features in terms of the staff development which they can assist. Let me take each feature in turn:

User-friendly style

Open learning text (whether in modules or on screens) tends to be informal and 'warm'. Sentences are short. Long words are avoided when shorter words do equally well. Most good teachers when chatting informally to one of their learners are equally warm. But what happens in more formal environments such as lectures or classrooms? We put on an act. We give a performance. We wish to demonstrate beyond doubt our professional status. (Perhaps you are not like this yourself, but you'll admit it's a common attitude.)

We have been educated and conditioned to think that the more sophisticated our language is, the more impressive we can be. We have been trained to regard informal writing as 'sloppy' and not worthy of our profession. But in many cases the formal language which we have considered so admirable, impedes communication rather than assisting it. What could be more important in any teaching/learning environment than good communication – both ways?

Close encounters with open learning make us focus sharply on the qualities of good communication. We begin to talk more easily rather than 'perform'. Our written materials (handouts, papers and so on) begin to convey their messages more effectively. Surely this is an important staff development achievement? But how many of us would have gone voluntarily to a staff development event entitled 'Stop taking ego-trips at the expense of your learners'?

'Personal' involvement of learners

This dimension obviously overlaps with user-friendliness. However, I'd like us to think particularly about the word 'you'. When you read it, it tends to have quite a powerful effect. You feel involved. You feel that the printed page (or screen) is addressing you as an individual. Similarly, the pronoun 'I'. But how many of us write our handouts or papers in terms of 'you' and 'I'? We've been trained to believe that third-person-passive writing is more professional. We find it helps us to sound more detached. I'm all for being objective, but I don't see that meaning that I've got to be detached.

Purposes clearly identified and explained

Good quality open learning materials contain clear statements of what the user should expect to be able to do at the end of each part. These are often stated in terms of objectives. Clear objectives help open learners discover:

- *what* they should become able to do
- *to what standard* they need to do it
- *how* they should do it.

What about conventional education and training? Syllabus content is often expressed in terms of objectives. But how often are these objectives placed firmly on our learners' agenda? I've even come across staff with the following view (though they wouldn't put it in these words): 'I don't show my learners the objectives; I don't want them to know which bits of the course I'm not going to cover.' Or: 'Why should I reveal this much detail? My learners should be able to tell for themselves what they need to do.'

Objectives are a great help to open learners. They spell out performance criteria. They explain the rules of the game. Surely this sort of information is of value to *any* sort of learner?

Close encounters with open learning help teaching staff keep clear objectives on their agenda. It's not usually that they didn't know how to *write* them; it's structuring the teaching/learning environment so that learners achieve them that matters. This is all the more probable when teachers and learners *share* ownership of objectives.

Activity-based systems

A key characteristic of open learning material is that the user is kept active. In text-based packages, there is rarely a double-page spread that isn't broken by something for the learner to do. In computer-based systems, the learner is kept even more active – usually in decision-making mode of some form.

Compare this activity-based approach with the average 'taught' session in a classroom or lecture theatre. The average lecture seems to be based on the 'transmit-receive' model. For much of the time learners simply watch, listen, and write down some of the things they see and hear (often less than adequately). Think about watching, listening and copying: they're very *passive* activities compared to problem-solving, decision-making, and answering questions – or even guessing answers. The latter types of activity are much more productive.

What about assessment? What do we *measure* when we set exams? Certainly not learners' ability to watch, listen or copy things down! We try to measure what they can *do* with what they *know*. The best way to learn anything is to *practise* doing it. Exams test people's ability to *answer questions* of one sort or another. So how much better it is to use much of the time we spend with our learners in situations where they can practise things, instead of leaving them to go and do all their practice on their own.

People who've been involved in open learning very often extend activity-based principles into their traditional teaching. They replace straight handouts by interactive handouts (see Chapter 10) which are *used* by learners *during* lectures. Straight handouts tend to be *filed* by learners after lectures, and hardly used at all.

Above all, when staff have been involved in open learning, many traditional lectures are turned into *learning* experiences; the lecturer becomes a facilitator instead of a mere transmitter of information.

Emphasis on processes rather than content

Traditionally, more attention has been paid to the details of syllabus content than to thinking about the processes by which learners get to grips with such content. Many (but sadly not all) staff who have been involved in open learning soon upgrade the priority of processes. Learning processes become the centre of attention. Teaching processes then become seen as means to an end – that of ensuring that learning processes are successful and efficient. 'What do my learners *do* during my lectures?' becomes a key question, replacing 'What shall I deliver during my lectures?'

If one were to advertise a staff development workshop on 'Making better use of your lecture time', who would come? A few new staff, and a few dedicated ones maybe! The ones who *need* to think about their teaching strategies would probably regard such a workshop as threatening – or even an insult to their professionalism. Getting involved in open learning is less threatening – yet it has huge payoffs in staff development terms.

It can of course be argued that the people who seek involvement in developments such as open learning are those who are receptive to ideas for improving their day-to-day teaching.

Feedback on success or problems

At the heart of all good open learning materials are self-assessment questions of one kind or another. They may not always be given this name, but they achieve a self-assessment purpose. As we explored in Chapter 3, the key ingredient in achieving this purpose is the 'response' that the learner receives after having a go at a question or activity.

Suppose a learner has made an attempt at a self-assessment question. He or she needs to know the following:

- Was I right?
- If not, what *is* the correct answer and what should I do to correct my error?

The open learner may well make mistakes. Getting things wrong is part of the process. Falling into traps is on the agenda. But how useful is it to make mistakes?

Reasons why making mistakes in open learning can be *beneficial* include the following:

- the mistakes are made *in private* – much less threatening than in public
- the learner finds out *why* the mistake was made
- the learner (in good materials) is made to feel that it was *useful* to have identified the trouble spot
- we all learn from our mistakes!

Some staff involved in open learning become rather expert at setting 'gentle traps' to allow learners to discover for themselves where their likely danger areas lie. Open learning writers also become expert at talking learners out of traps they've fallen into. Questions are often designed *because* quite a few learners will get it wrong. Having made their mistakes in private, they are unlikely to make the same ones when later they face public assessment such as exams.

Traditional teaching tends to be based on the idea that you tell them as much as you can, then hope that the good learners will get it right. Open learning looks much more closely at what causes learners trouble, and how best we can help learners who get things wrong.

This principle of allowing learners to learn from their mistakes can easily be extended to classroom teaching. Self-assessment questions can be posed in the classroom. Responses can be displayed on a screen or issued in print. Learners can still retain some of the privacy – they can assess their own answers individually, without their tutor probing too deeply into who got what right. Alternatively, learners can *share* their experience of getting things wrong – alleviating any feelings of failure.

A staff development workshop on 'Designing self-assessment exercises for learners to use in your lectures' would attract only the dedicated minority of teachers. Many staff would feel threatened by the implied criticism of their current methods. Yet staff who have used (or written) open learning materials will often spontaneously begin to use self-assessment activities as a normal part of the learning process – in the classrooms and in homework.

Learning styles firmly on the agenda

Getting involved in open learning helps one realize that each learner learns in his or her own way. Study skills become a definite item on the agenda. In some areas of higher and further education, study skills have received attention for some time. Open learners have additional study skills needs, and staff who become involved in open learning become increasingly aware of the range of study skills needed by learners. These needs are best responded to by the subject teacher, rather than by an outside study skills guide. That said, there remains the need for more subject teachers to get involved in study skills work.

The most caring of those staff who tutor open learners find that they extend their help regarding study skills development to conventional learners too. All learners benefit from help regarding how best to *manage* their studies. This sort of development of learners' transferrable skills is increasingly seen as important. For example, it is relevant to BTEC's Programme of Integrative Assignments and to the Training Agency's work developing Enterprise skills.

Enhanced communication skills

Dealing with learners at a distance can help to develop the communication skills of teaching staff. Such staff may well be already advanced in face-to-face skills, and handling groups of learners. However, teaching staff also need good written communication skills (for example when composing handout material, or communicating good practice with colleagues elsewhere through academic papers). The development of these skills, effected by tutoring distance learners, can play an important part in conventional teaching.

Practice at dealing with individuals

One thing that anyone involved in open or distance learning learns very quickly is to treat each student as an individual. The same sort of treatment is equally desirable in face-to-face encounters. Staff who have realized the importance of treating learners as individual people rather than faces in a throng find that they can extend the benefits of a more personal approach. This enhances learner motivation as well as learning effectiveness.

Peer-group interaction

So far in this chapter, I've been stressing the benefits of open and distance learning. It is time to set the record straight – there are disadvantages too! The primary disadvantage experienced by learners working on their own is the lack of peer group interaction.

In conventional educational environmentss, learners learn a lot from each other. They also benefit from the comfort of finding that they have problems in common with each other. If everyone in a group is having difficulty with Mr Jones' thermodynamics course, learners feel less threatened by the problem.

The most caring of staff involved in supporting open learning find many ways of trying to compensate for the lack of peer interaction. This has the important result that they become more aware of how best they can use the peer group interaction possibilities with conventional classes and groups.

Conclusions

I have tried to outline the sorts of staff development that can be affected by getting involved in open or distance learning. It has to be admitted, however, that I've been thinking about staff who play the role of pathfinders rather than those who have more run-of-the-mill involvement. But simply getting involved in something new can inspire a run-of-the-mill teacher to become a pathfinder.

I have also tried to show that such staff development often occurs covertly rather than overtly. This means there is less resistance to changes in approach or attitude. It also means that processes become regarded as more important, and subject content ceases to be the centre of attention. Since most teaching staff are professionals who have already got the content more-or-less right, the move towards emphasis on teaching/learning processes seems to me to be a very positive stride in the right direction.

15. Workshops That Work

I've spent much of my time in the last ten years designing, running and evaluating workshops. Many of these have been to help to develop open learning authors, editors, tutors – and learners themselves. Some of the workshops have been three-day residential events, others have been one-day events.

But what is a workshop? How is it different from a seminar? *Is* it different? That's what this final chapter is about. I've included it in this book because I believe that workshops can be an effective, efficient, and cost-effective way of developing people's skills and ideas. I wish to share with you some of the experience I have picked up from my successes – and failures – running workshops.

A specimen workshop programme

Let's start with a case study. Here's one of my programmes for a workshop, with the title 'Workshops that Work!'

Workshops that Work

Workshop Aim

Workshops can be used for many kinds of development with teaching staff and with students. This workshop is to identify criteria by which to ensure that workshop programmes and processes achieve their objectives.

Workshop Objectives

By the end of the workshop, you will have:

1. explored the use of Workshop Objectives.
2. examined the value of modifying workshop objectives in the light of participants' expectations.
3. developed a checklist of criteria to ensure that workshop processes are productive.

4. discussed the timetabling of workshop programmes in a way that maintains flexibility and responsiveness.
5. experimented with techniques to evaluate workshops (in formative and summative ways).
6. identified some advantages of well designed workshops over other forms of teaching/learning/training.

Number of Participants: maximum 16

Facilities Required

- room with moveable seating
- overhead projector
- OHP pens and acetates for participants' use
- flipchart and pens.

This programme is for a short workshop – a mere half-day event. I did not produce a minute-by-minute timetable for the workshop – that would have imposed inflexibility on what was intended to be a sharing of experience, and gathering of wisdom!

A specimen discussion paper

I did, however, prepare a discussion paper, which I present as the main 'ingredient' in this chapter. As you'll see, in this particular instance the paper is designed to be given to participants towards the end of (or after) the event.

'Workshops that Work': some pre-workshop thoughts

The purpose of this workshop is to share experiences, and develop criteria together. I have prepared this short paper in advance of the workshop, based on my own experiences of designing and conducting workshops. I hope it may be useful to issue it towards the end of the workshop (not at the start, in case it were to polarize discussions on the issues I happen to have addressed). I will be even more pleased if the products of participants at this workshop completely eclipse the thoughts below!

Workshops: some definitions

'A workshop is a group event where each participant emerges able to do things better than he/she could at the start of the workshop.'

'A workshop is an event where each participant actively contributes for most of the time.'

'A workshop is an event where participants learn a lot from each other.'

'The outcomes of a workshop are dependent on the contributions of participants, rather than on input from the leader.'

'A workshop is not a lecture or a seminar, though it may include short episodes in such modes.'

The aim of this workshop is to identify criteria which may help ensure that workshop programmes and processes achieve their objectives. I've listed below various criteria under a range of headings relating to principal features of workshop programmes. First I consider general issues common to most workshops. At the end I include some general recommendations based on experience.

Uses of workshop objectives

Here are some of the purposes that workshop objectives can serve.

- to help ensure that the right people come to the workshop. (When workshop objectives are known in advance, participants who can already achieve them are able to see that they may have little reason to attend.)
- to help focus participants' attention on the main purposes of the workshop
- to assist in the planning of the timing of workshop components

Participant modification of workshop objectives

Getting participants involved in formulating or refining workshop objectives is a useful way of fine-tuning the detail of a workshop to meet participants' needs and wishes. Here are some suggestions regarding how this may be done.

1. It may be best (when possible) to allow participants-to-be to plan workshop objectives from the start (eg it may be possible to arrange a pre-workshop event, or at the end of workshop 1 to plan for workshop 2 and so on).
2. Collecting participants' expectations provides a means for fine-tuning workshop objectives to meet the needs of a group.
3. If objectives are visibly modified to take into account participants' expectations, the group will feel more 'ownership' of the event. Participants are then more likely to follow up the workshop in terms of trying out ideas and practices.

Draft checklist for workshop processes

At a successful workshop, the processes used are at least as important as the content that is covered. Here are some ideas regarding processes.

1. Can the workshop be accelerated (and participants' experience brought to a common starting point) by issuing a pre-workshop task? (The completed task can be supplied to the workshop leader before the event, and the workshop tailored to take on board matters arising from the ways participants approached the task.)
2. Especially with participants who don't already know each other, it's useful to have a relevant, non-threatening 'ice-breaker' to get them talking to each other.
3. A U-shape works much better than rows. Participants need to be able to see each others' faces.
4. Are workshop processes participant-centred, rather than 'leader-led'? (If you're leading a workshop, it's worth asking yourself this every few minutes!)
5. Is there a good mixture of activities, including appropriate use of individual work, work in pairs and small groups, individual/group report-back, brainstorming (oral, acetate, paper and so on)?

6. Does 'input' from the workshop leader take a minimum proportion of the time available? For example, is handout material used to avoid lengthy expositions?
7. Where participants have generated material/ideas, are these then 'crystallized' and circulated to participants (eg by 'workshop products' being produced from participants' acetates and flipcharts)? Are 'workshop products' produced and circulated quickly?
8. Is it possible to ask what participants think of the workshop without waiting till the end of the event? A quick round-the-table response to 'How are you feeling about things so far?' can be most valuable – if sometimes terrifying!
9. When dividing participants into syndicates of 2, 3 or 4, it is useful deliberately to 'mix' them. Syndicates formed spontaneously from participants who happened to be sitting together (and probably already know each other) are in general less interesting than ones where participants are 'strangers'.
10. If there are one or two 'negative' participants, it's worth rearranging syndicates for each task, so that the negative influence is spread out, rather than being concentrated on a few unfortunate (positive) participants.

Some timetabling considerations

It's important that participants feel their time has been used *wisely* and *productively*. Here are some general suggestions regarding the planning of workshop schedules.

1. Participants like to see timings and content details for various sections of a workshop. However, they become restless if the workshop is seen to be running behind schedule. Therefore plan timings carefully, so that the probability of being able to adhere to them is maximized. For instance, include two or three parts in a 'slot' so that if one part overruns, the remaining parts can be squeezed slightly.
2. Always finish on time (coffee, lunch, close of workshop). Participants may become quite negative if the workshop overruns.
3. If, near the scheduled close of an event, much remains to be done, use the time left to arrange a follow-up (including its draft objectives). Alternatively, allow an optional continuation after a break (letting those with trains to catch or kids to collect slip out quietly and informally).
4. Start on time. This is necessary to avoid alientating those who have arrived promptly. But, don't start with anything on which everything else will depend – those who arrive late would be permanently disadvantaged (and may become hostile/unproductive). Therefore plan something useful – but not essential – for the first half-hour or so.
5. A 30-minute coffee-break with a punctual return is better than a 15-minute coffee break from which participants straggle back for several minutes.
6. If an issue comes up which may mean major departures from the timetable, negotiate a programme change/substitution with participants (rather than squeeze it in and run late).

Evaluation of workshops

Real evaluation of workshops is likely to be achievable only months or years after the event, when it may be possible to analyse what participants did as a result of things they got out of a workshop. However, it is possible to obtain *feedback* in a number of ways.

- *questionnaires:* these can contain parts for general views (eg boxes to tick) and spaces for specific responses (eg the two most useful element of the workshop were ...).
- *oral feedback:* this can be gathered during or after a workshop. One problem is that the findings can be coloured by politeness and wishes not to disagree with the consensus view of others attending.
- *feedback from workshop leaders:* it is often useful to address the question: 'What would you do differently if conducting the same workshop tomorrow with a new group of participants?'
- *feedback from participants' bosses:* when it is possible to gather feedback from people such as supervisors, heads of department, and so on, such feedback often has the advantage of including things which the participants would have been reluctant to give directly to the workshop leader.
- *post-workshop feedback:* it is sometimes possible to gather participants' 'considered' reactions to a workshop – for example some weeks after the event.

Advantages of workshops over other training strategies

The advantages may include the following:

1. Workshops should be more open-ended than other kinds of training event, so can be altered to meet new needs arising, or participants' expectations and wishes.
2. Participants emerge from a good workshop with the feeling that they have contributed actively, and that they share ownership of the outcomes of the workshop. They are then more likely to build on what they have done.
3. Workshop situations can be used for role-play and simulation, in a non-threatening environment. Participants can, for example, rehearse how they might best respond to difficult situations, or try out controversial approaches, and gain feedback from fellow participants.
4. If participants are kept active, it is usual for them to be able to gain at least as much from each other as from the workshop leader or workshop resource materials.
5. When a workshop is repeated with new groups, the workshop leader can cross-fertilize findings from previous workshops. This helps ensure that all possible dimensions are included in analyses and discussions.
6. To some extent, workshops can be 'open learning experiences' for participants, who can, within reason, learn at their own pace and in their own way.

General recommendations

Number of participants
Six to 16 works well. If there are more than 20 participants, it is likely that participants do not feel that they are involved sufficiently actively (report-backs can become boring, and so on). If there are less than six participants, the experience base is rather too limited.

- For 16 or more participants, it is desirable to have more than one leader so that participants can be split into smaller groups for most activities.

Co-leaders
1. Never work at short notice with someone you've not worked with before.
2. If you want to have an 'equal' co-leader, it's best to have someone you've worked with several times already.
3. Co-leaders are best trained by 'assisting' you on two or three workshops.

4. New workshop repertoire is best gained by assisting an expert in the field concerned on two or three occasions before launching out on your own.

Things to arrange in advance
When dealing with the person on-site who is responsible for organizing your workshop, it's always worth mentioning in writing things like overhead projector, flipchart, room with moveable seating, extra rooms for syndicate work, timings of coffee/lunch and so on.

Things to have with you
It's generally useful to have the following:

- acetate sheets and overhead projection pens
- place cards
- five or so *extra* copies of any handouts to be used
- Blu-tack
- spare copies of the workshop programme.

So what actually happened at the workshop?

You've seen the workshop objectives, and the discussion paper given to participants. So how have such workshops actually gone? To cut a long story short, the issues mentioned in the paper above were addressed by participants (variously working singly, in pairs, in syndicates and as a larger group). Participants' ideas were captured on pieces of acetate and flipcharts, and were discussed and argued about. By the end of the workshop, almost everything in my paper had been 'discovered' by participants, who left the workshop with the feeling of ownership of the various criteria proposed, and with my paper reminding them of the things that *they* had thought of.

A specimen open-learning workshop programme

One of the resource papers we used at the workshop was a workshop outline programme that I have frequently employed when working with open learning writers. I normally use such an outline as a basis for discussion with clients for whom I run workshops. The programmes then are fine-tuned to the particular needs of the participants to be involved – and may look considerably more detailed than the outline below. At workshops I've run on 'Workshops that Work', outlines such as that below have provided a useful basis for criticism and discussion.

Writing open learning materials

Forty-eight-hour workshop, for participants who have previously attended one of my one-day workshops on 'Exploring Open Learning', and who wish to write their own open learning materials).

Workshop Objectives

By the end of the workshop you should be able to:

- use learning objectives to the advantage of open learners
- compose self-assessment questions and responses, as key ingredients in open learning modules
- develop a user-friendly tone and style, suitable for people working on their own
- adopt an efficient strategy for planning and writing open learning materials.

Outline Programme

Day 1
1400   Arrive and register
1430   Introduction, workshop expectations
1500   Introductory exercise
1530   Tea
1600   Review of principles and practices of open learning materials and systems
1700   Analysis of samples of existing open learning materials
1730   Input: objectives and Open Learners
1800   Break
1830   Dinner
1930   Exercises on composing objectives for open learners
2100   Close of day 1

Day 2
0800   Breakfast
0900   Input: on the design of self-assessment questions and responses. Discussion.
1000   Exercises and report-back sessions on the development of SAQs and responses.
1230   Lunch
1330   Input: Tone and Style for Open Learning Materials Discussion.
1430   Exercises and report-back sessions on writing text
1600   Input: on Strategies for Writing Open Learning Materials Discussion.
1700   General discussion, and briefing for evening task
1730   Close of formal programme for Day 2.
1830   Dinner
(individual work during evening)

Day 3
0800   Breakfast
0900   Report-back and analysis of work done by participants overnight
1100   General discussion
1130   Study-skills development of open learners
1200   Workshop review

1230   Lunch
1330   Disperse

Facilities needed
OHP, flipchart, acetate sheets and OHP pens for participant use. Room with moveable seating, U-shape arrangement initially.

Participants
Suggested number: 12; maximum number: 16; minimum number: 8.

Conclusions

I hope this final chapter has given you some ideas of how workshops can be used to develop the skills that people need when they move into open learning – whether as writers, tutors or in other ways. I trust you'll also find my suggestions for the design of workshop sessions compatible with the 'activity' based nature of my recommendations for all aspects of open learning.

Index

adult entry 124–8
aims 33, 35
assessment 105, 128, 138
assessment
   criteria 87–9, 128
   objectives 36
assignment design 63
assignments 81–90, 92–7
   purposes of 82
audio 67

background material 28
benefits of open learning 98–104

checklists 65, 135
choosing open learning materials 135–9
CMAs 92–7
colour 71
communication skills 75–7, 110–14, 145
completion questions 55
computer-based material 67
computer-marked assignments (CMAs)
   92–7
content versus processes 116, 143–4
copy editing 129
cost-effectiveness 18
counselling 105–14

diagrams 66, 137
distance learning 14

editing open learning materials 129–33
educational editing 129–33
ego-trips 21

face-to-face teaching 26–31, 115–23,
   140–46
face-to-face tutoring 114
fault-finding questions 56
features of open learning 21–5, 98, 141
feedback
   from learners 94, 128

to learners 24, 82, 84, 144–5
(written) checklist 112
filling in blanks 52–3
flags 70

grades 82–4

handouts 115–23
   advantages 118
   disadvantages 118
headings 70
housestyle 61, 129
   editing 129

illustrations 66, 137
indenting 71
interaction 135–6, *see also* SAQs
interactive
   audio 67
   handouts 115–23
   processes 118–20
   video 67
learner
   choice 15
   profiles 107
learners' feelings 103, 107–9, 125
learning styles 145
lecturers 17, 115–23, 140–46
lectures 115–23
   problems of 115, 117–18, 120–21
letters from tutors 111–12
live sessions 17, 115–23, 147–54

marking schemes 87–9
marks or scores 82–4
matching questions 51–2
media
   checklist 68
   usage 67, 68, 137–8
modified Fog Index 78–9
motivation 21
multiple choice 47–51, 92–3, 94–7

negative feelings 109
non-print media 67, 137–8

objectives 23, 33–41, 71, 99, 131, 136, 142
    checklist 40–41
    design of 36
    mapping out 38
    usefulness to learners 38–40
open 14
    learning, introduction to 14

package 15
peer-group interaction 146
phone manner 113
photographs 66
practical kits 67

questions 21, 42–59, 101, 131, 136

responses 92, 95–7
responses to SAQs 42–59, 131–2, 136
reviews 24, 65, 132

SAQ
    design 62
    quality checklist 57–9
    responses 42–59, 131–2, 136
    response, design 62
    response, role 43–6
    types 46–7
SAQs 42–59, 101, 131, 136
science, adult entry to 124–8
scores or marks 82–4, 93
selection of materials 135–9
self-assessment questions 42–59, 131
self-esteem 21
sequencing questions 54
signposting 61, 69
sponsors 100–102
    attitudes of 103
staff development 140–46
study skills 24, 137
style 75–80
summaries 24, 65, 132

syllabus-objectives 36

tables of data 66
tape/slide 67
taxonomies 34
teaching 140–46
technical editing 129
technology, adult entry to 124–8
telephone communication 113
telephone tutoring 113
TMA design checklist 85–6
TMAs 81–90
    importance of 86–7
tone and style 23, 75–80, 132–3, 136
traditional textbooks 21–5
trainer development 140–46
training workshops 147–54
transmit-receive model 116, 143
tutor marked assignments 81–90
tutoring 105–14, 127
    checklist 110
tutors' feelings 103

user-friendliness 75–80, 136–7, 141–2

video 67, 137–8
visual material 23, 66, 71, 137

white space 23, 71
workshop
    objectives 147, 149
    programmes 152–4
    timetabling 150
workshops, advantages of 151
workshops (training) 147–54
writing
    introductions 65
    objectives 62
    open learning materials workshop 153–4
    strategies 60–73
    text 62, 64
written
    communication 110–11
    feedback checklist 112